Let My Words Be Sweet Upon You

Messages from Grandmother God

Let My Words Be Sweet Upon You

Messages from Grandmother God

by

Emma Hild Hofstede

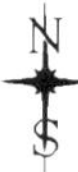

NORTH STAR PRESS OF ST. CLOUD, INC.

St. Cloud, Minnesota

ISBN-10: 0-87839-339-0
ISBN-13: 978-0-87839-339-8

Printed in the United States of America

Published by
North Star Press of St. Cloud, Inc.
PO Box 451
St. Cloud, Minnesota 56302

northstarpress.com

Dedication

*To my husband, Al, my daughter Emily, son-in-law Michael,
my son Al, and my daughter-in-law Kimberly*

Acknowledgements

Since Grandmother God arrived, I have been her scribe. I would e-mail the writings to the Grandmother God Team as they were written, and they would send back their comments and encouragement.

Grandmother God wanted her thoughts and ideas to be available to everyone. Her message is one of pure love. What you have in this book are her beautiful thoughts put into writings. They are messages of love to you, dear reader.

Grandmother God's Team:

Mary Anderson	Janet Benskin
Nora Collins	Connie Draves
Marsha Gould	Michele Helgen
Barbara Keffer	Michele Krakowski
Greg & Julie Larson	Tess Nelson
Delores Olson	Sister Ruth Roland, OP

My husband listened to each one of the writings. I am deeply grateful to him for his continued words of encouragement and love.

Mary Anderson, Grandmother God, Tess Nelson, and I worked together as the initial team. As we listened to each other, ideas flourished. Diane Odash joined our team as a copy-editor. She added her talent and enthusiasm to the group. With the expertise of those at North Star Press, we now have the book you are holding in your hands. From all of us we say, "Enjoy!"

Introduction

Dear Reader,

Two years ago my husband was diagnosed with a life-threatening cancer and our lives changed forever. It felt like falling into a parallel universe where everything looked the same, but could not have been more different. From deep within my own belief system I knew that incredible transformation is possible during difficult times. When you suffer one of life's few truly painful experiences – the death or illness of a loved one – you usually take one of two paths. You can let your love grow within yourself and within your loved one, or you can become bitter and focus only on the unfairness of this degree of suffering. I knew that down deep because of the love and sacrifice that would be required during this period of pain and adversity, that it held the unique possibility of creating a stronger connection between my husband and me.

What I did not know was that turning toward this love would ultimately result in a series of writings and drawings about God, but that is exactly what happened. It was like a crack opened in the earth and a stream of creativity flowed forth from me. When I dipped into this stream, what I pulled out was an image of God so loving and beautiful that I began writing and drawing her. This was no ordinary notion of God that I had grown up with and had believed in for most of my adult life. This was the awareness of God as a feminine figure, a comforting being, who bakes pies, enjoys gardening, has a whimsical sense of humor, and consoled me through some of my darkest moments. This was my Grandmother God.

I sincerely believe that the creative force that sustained me during this time of pain and confusion is a force that flows within all of us. We dip into this river when the time is right. I would hope that there are easier ways to enter this stream besides suffering, but just knowing that it is there may help you during your own life experiences.

This book is about unconditional love. It contains a promise of hope that within each of our lives there is a potential for our own radiant spirits to burst forth in an expression of creativity and beauty.

I hope you enjoy Grandmother God's book.

Emma Hofstede
Friend & Scribe

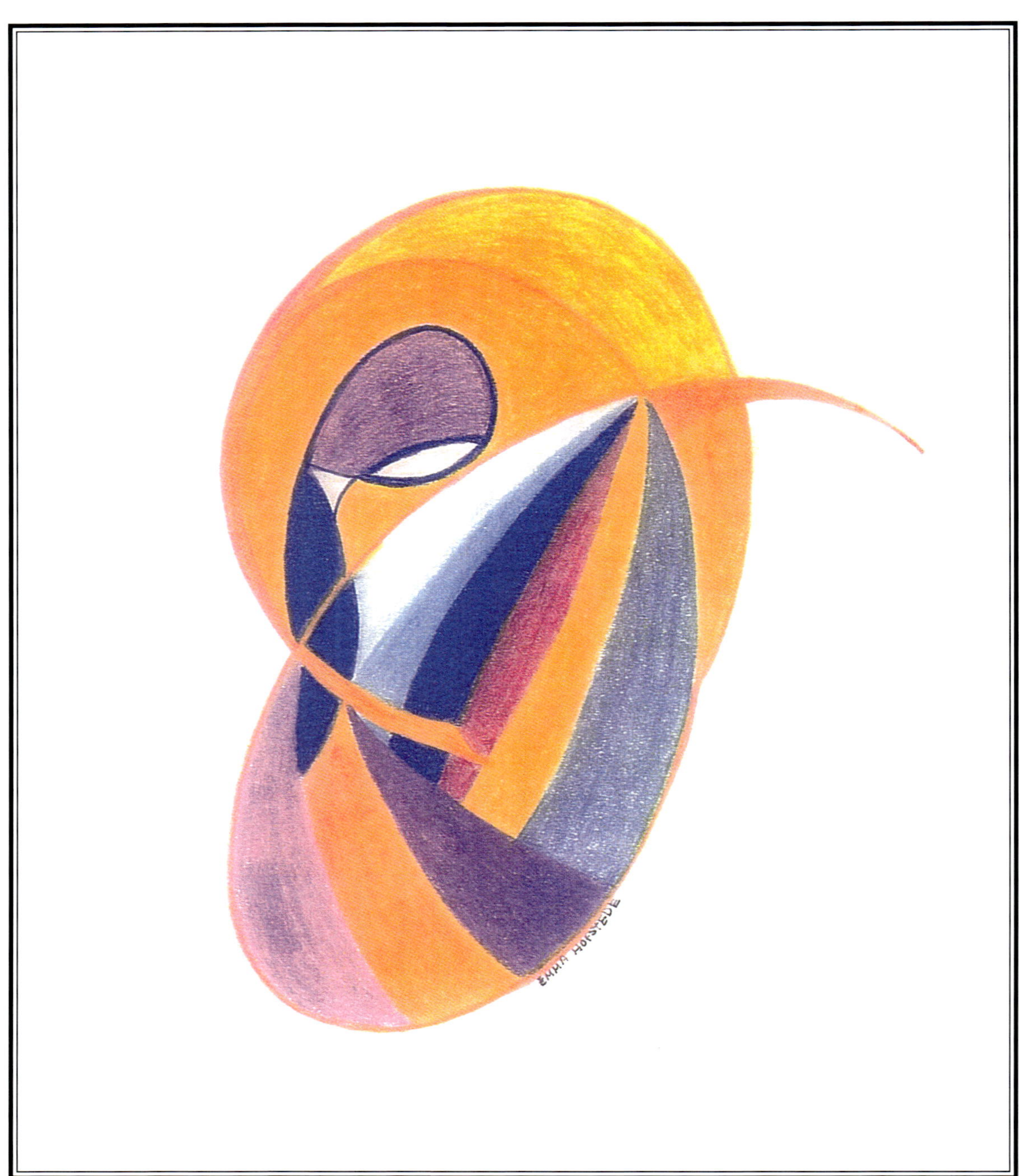

SCRIBE

Let My Words Be Sweet Upon You

Messages from Grandmother God

Prologue

THE INNER ROOM

Inside me there is a room where Grandmother God lives. I know this because I would cease to exist if this wasn't true. She fills the space with swirling colors of energy and light. I can see them under the door. I love going there to spend time with her. When I am with her everything changes. The world falls away and I can breathe easily the pure air of love. Nothing I do upsets her, and no matter how fearful I get, she understands how hard life has been for me this past year. I tell her that I can't do it anymore, this constant worrying about my husband. She says, "Come Sweetheart, sit down and let's talk."

She is my Grandmother God.

Sometimes she has tea, and sometimes something sweet to eat. She holds and rocks me and tells me how much I am loved, and that she will never leave me.

I asked her how I could feel her presence, and she said she would teach me her ways. She is beautiful. I could spend the rest of my life with her and be completely happy. When I get really scared I forget about her living inside of me. I wish I wouldn't.

The Inner Room is a place with glowing colors, and the air is filled with the sweet smell of night jasmine. You can meet your Grandmother God there any time you want.

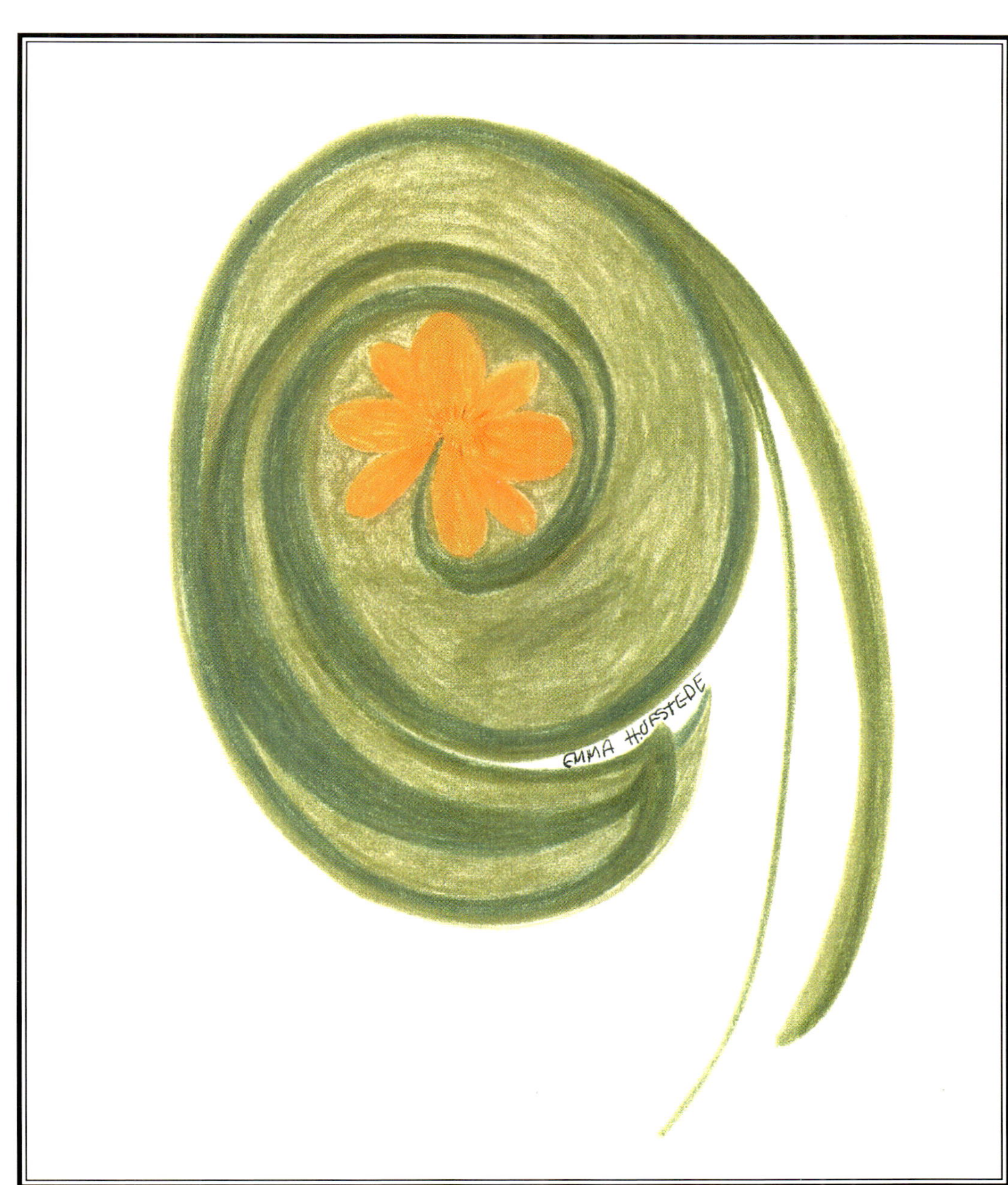

EMMA HOFSTEDE

The Hidden Lilies

Our shoreline at the lake cabin was restored to its natural habitat about ten years ago. Now it is in full bloom with honeysuckle bushes, birch and pine trees, and beautiful native flowers.

A few days ago we discovered, hidden among the high growth, a patch of golden lilies. There they were, in all the glory of lilydom. You had to push the grasses aside and peek in to see their glory. Grandmother God loved them. She would go and look at them and smile. I showed them to my neighbor as if we had something so special and beautiful to share.

Here's the story. A young family came to use our shore to fish. The two little children ran wild as though they were in a public park. As they were leaving, they discovered the lilies, uprooted them and ran. I cannot tell you how that affected us. It was a typical child thing to do, to pick flowers, but somehow it left us feeling sad.

I asked Grandmother God why she thought it touched us so deeply. She never has pat answers. She said, "Honey, close your eyes. Can you see the lilies? They are not gone; they are blooming inside of you." She said, "No one can take the beauty you have stored in your memory. Yes, it was fun to see them secretly growing there, but now they are hidden deep within you. There they are free to blow in the wind and give off their beautiful fragrance. They will never die or be uprooted from your heart." She remembered a quote she liked from John Keats, "A thing of beauty is a joy forever."

Grandmother God is like the lilies. She lives inside of you giving off the sweetness of her presence. She hides deep down in the crevices of your heart. To see her, just push aside whatever is hiding her, and there you will find your own Grandmother God bursting with golden lily love.

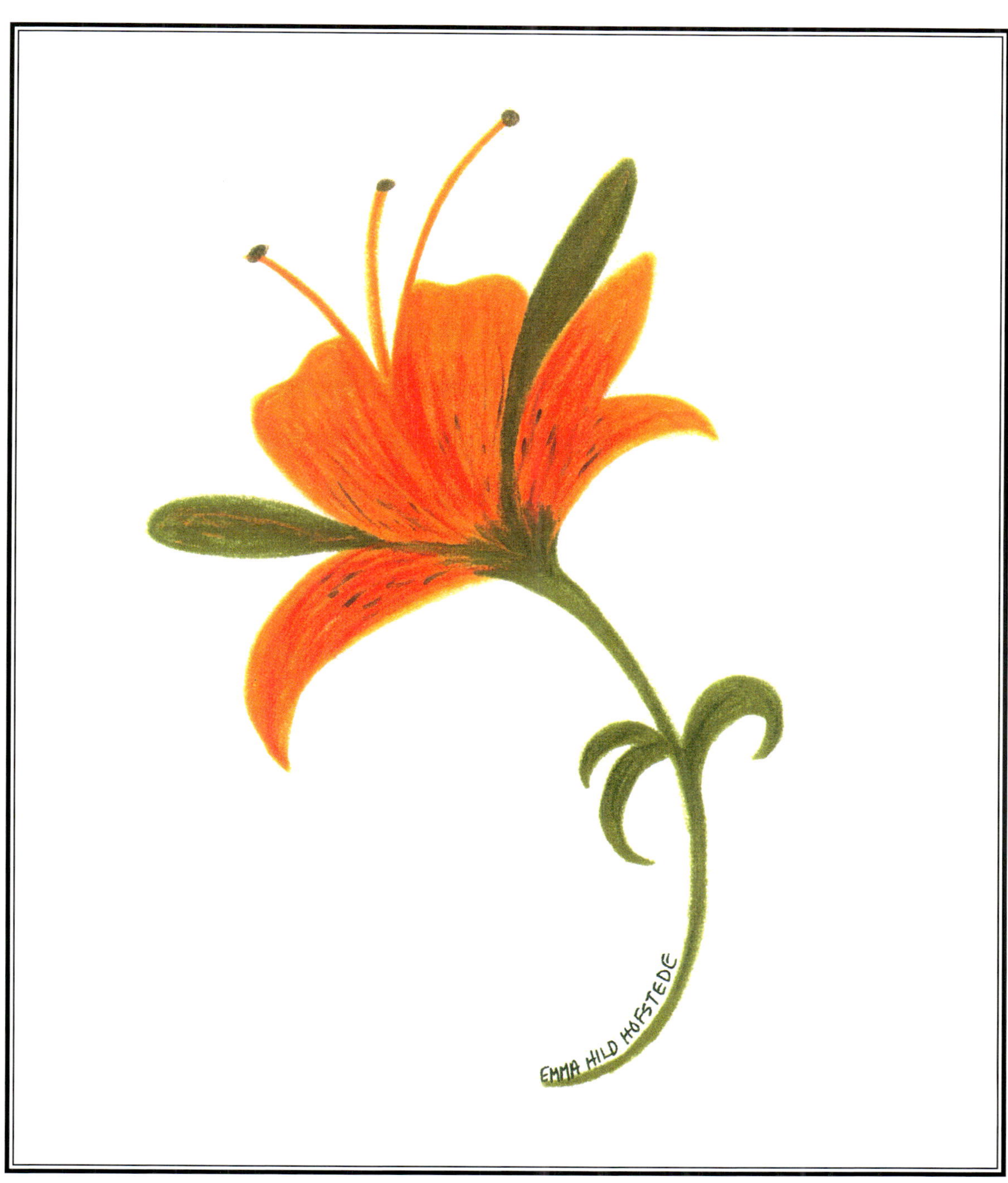

EMMA HILD HOFSTEDE

True Team Spirit

When Grandmother God watches the news, it feels like she goes some place far away. She gives her undivided attention to each person she sees. It is as if she knows them personally.

Last night we saw something on the evening news we will never forget. Two archrival women's softball teams were playing their championship game. I have to admit I did not get the details right away, as I tend to half listen to the news, but Grandmother God did. These are her people. A woman hit a game-winning home run, got injured, and could not finish running the bases. The game rules are that no one from her team could run them for her. So two of the opposing team's members carried her around the bases and her team won the game.

Grandmother God and I both cried. It reminded me of how God wants us to live our lives, carrying and being carried. Grandmother God just looked at me and an understanding flooded both of us. She knew I got it and so did I.

I am sure all of us have had times of being a carrier and being carried. Isn't this a beautiful story? If all of the news could have stories like this once in awhile, I would watch more attentively.

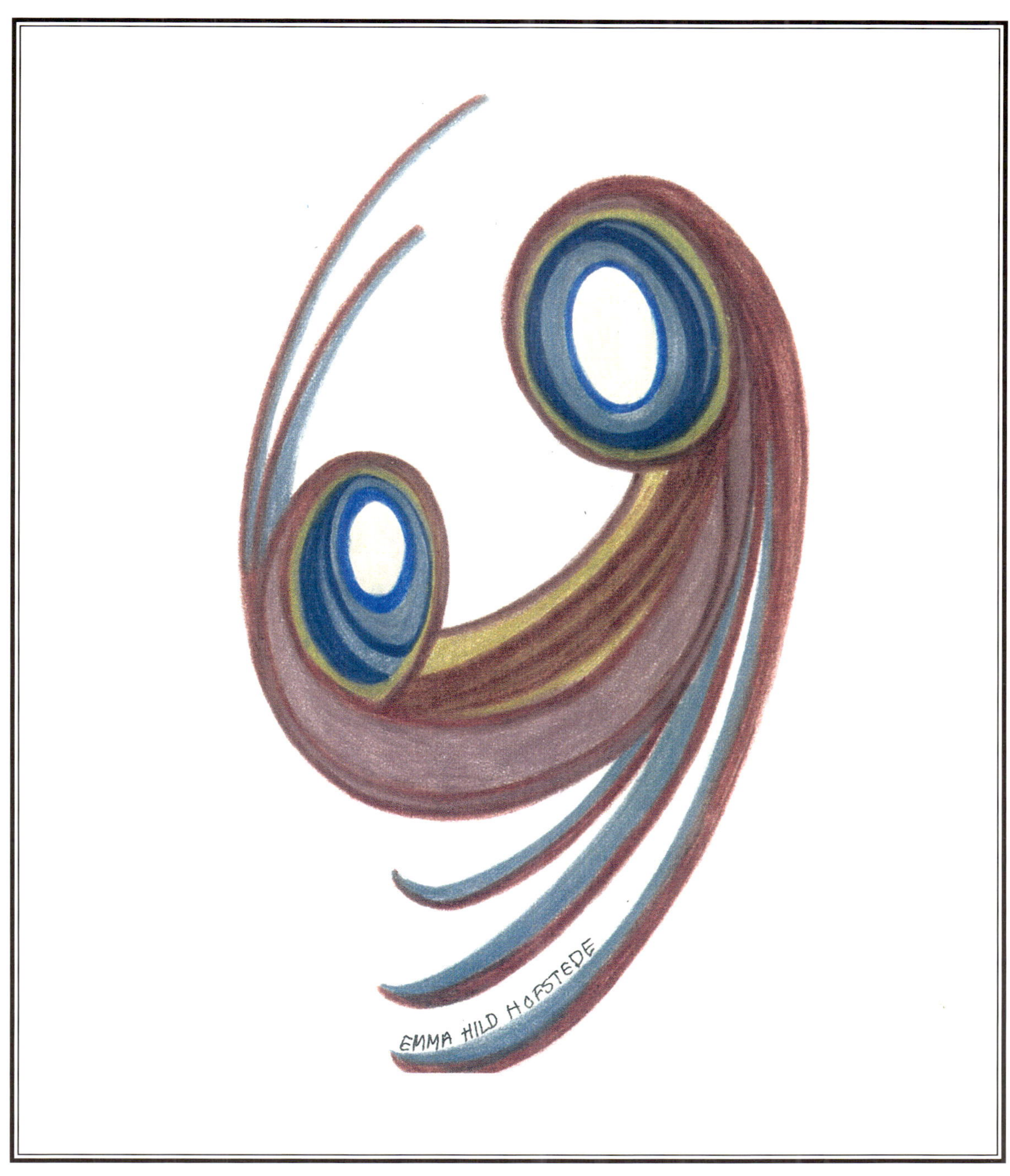

EMMA HILD HOFSTEDE

I Am Peace (Ani Shalom)

This morning we are having our tea and reading the Psalms. Each day we look for one that touches something inside of us. Today it was Psalm 120:

> "I am for peace, but when I speak, they
> are for war."

We just loved the idea of thinking of ourselves as peace. What a wonderful mantra for the day! I am peace.

What would it feel like to be peace? Grandmother God had to stop and think about this one. She is peace itself, but how would she describe that feeing?

She asked me what I thought it meant. After a few minutes I said, "Maybe the feeling of stillness, and courage or even fear, at the same time." I thought of Gandhi and Martin Luther King, and how they protested against injustice and violence. I would need to be centered in myself and unmovable in my belief that violence begets violence.

I asked Grandmother God how she would explain it. She said, "Honey, Ani Shalom, that is who I am." That means no harshness towards yourself, or anyone else in the whole universe. It is such a deep awareness of who you are, and who everyone else is, that you cannot be anything else but peace. When you can see God in everyone and everything, how could you hurt them? We are all God's beautiful creations, precious jewels. What blinds people to this reality is having experienced violence in their own lives. Because they did not have an experience of deep unconditional love early in life, they struggle all their lives with feeling unlovable.

"Ani Shalom," I am peace. What a gift to our world!

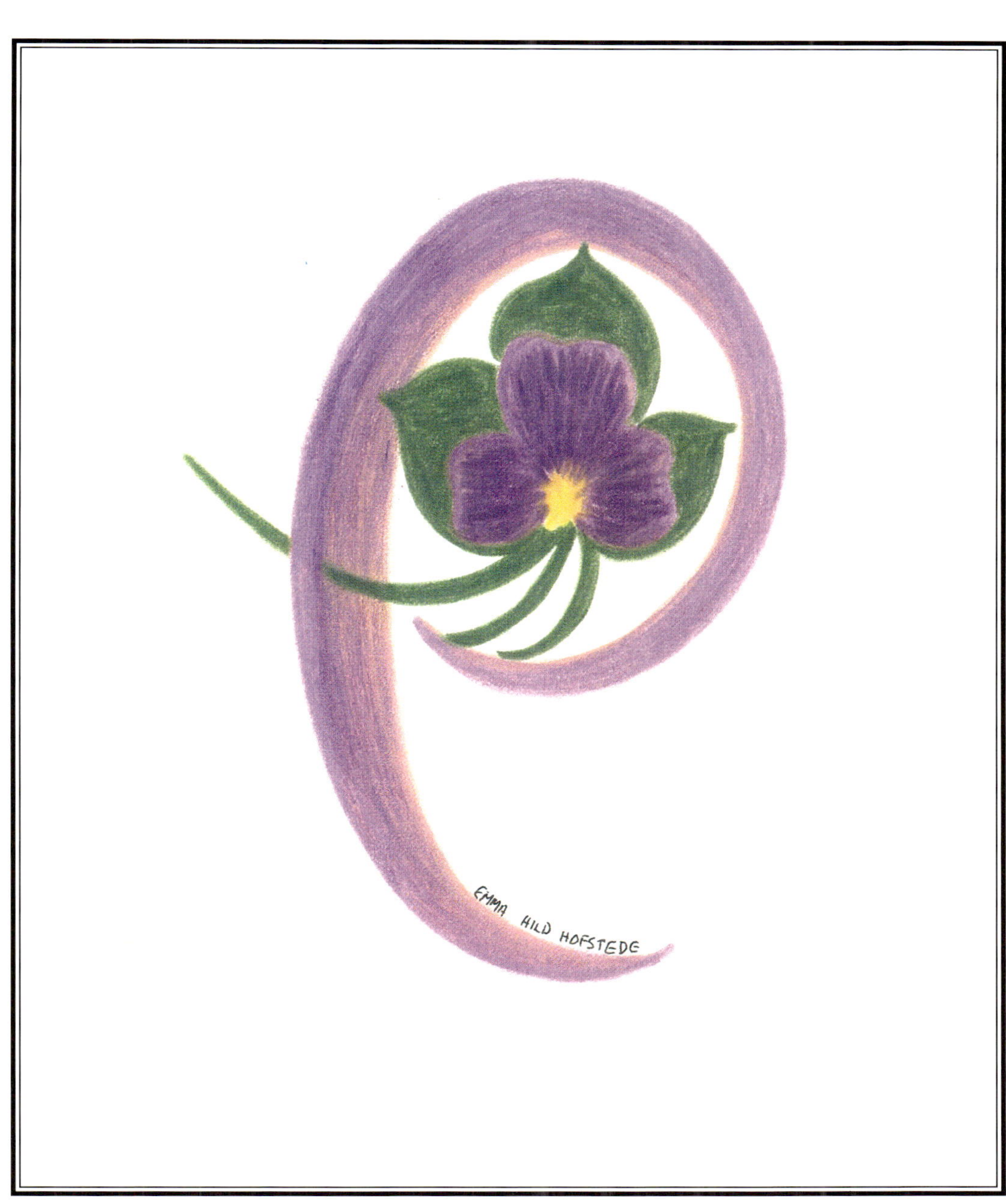
EMMA HILD HOFSTEDE

The Velveteen Rabbit

Grandmother God and I were sitting on our front porch today. I was telling her that I was so full of sad feelings that at the least hint of kindness I would start crying. She said, "Honey, it reminds me of the story about the Velveteen Rabbit." I started really crying then, isn't that lovely? I love that story. It took so much love, sickness and pain before the rabbit could become real; only then was she free to run in the woods and play with her rabbit friends. There is no other story that could have made me feel better. I have always loved that book, and somehow Grandmother God knew that. She is amazing. It helped me see that no matter what we have to go through in life, something wonderful can come out of it - freedom and being more real.

After feeling better, I was hungry for her delicious peach pie. I think she has a secret recipe, and uses only Colorado peaches. She made tea, and we enjoyed pie à la mode. She really knows something about how good pie can comfort you after sharing your feelings.

I am telling you, she is the best friend you could ever have. Her ability to love can make your "fur" fall off much faster. She is the most Real Grandmother God you could ever know. She listens with love, and then follows that with her delicious baking. She will fold you into her arms and you will feel her heavenly presence.

Invite her into your heart whenever you want. Time means nothing to her because she doesn't live in it. She will be with you as long as you like. She'll just be listening, loving and telling you how much she loves you.

She may even offer you some peach pie.

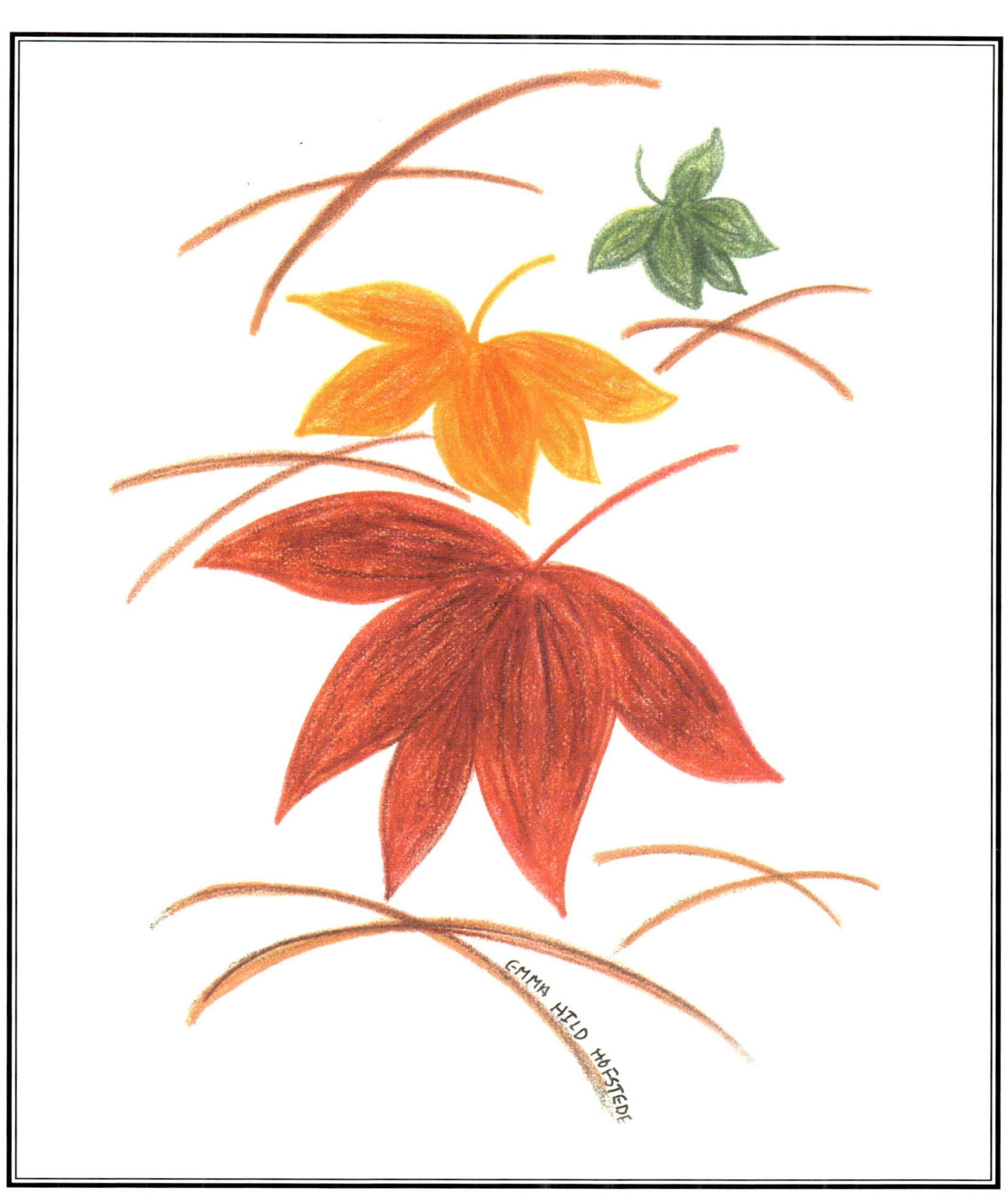

EMMA HILD HOFSTEDE

Overwhelming Love

Is it possible that you could be overwhelmed with love from God? There is a line in Psalm 114 where God turns flint to a stream of water.

> "Who turns the rock to a pond of water,
>   flint to a spring of water."

It is a metamorphic kind of love. Grandmother God and I have been contemplating that thought since this morning. She doesn't say much until I bring up the subject and ask her, "How could God overwhelm us with love?"

She just looked at me and said, "Oh Honey, you know how I love you and your family and friends. I have been telling you, showing you, spelling it out for you in so many different ways. The word "Overwhelming" may be a little strong. Think of it as a transformative love, like alchemy. If God can turn flint into a flowing stream, just think of what God can do with you.

"I have come here to show you this kind of love. I have a little different method than the God in the Psalms; I use flint to cut cakes and pies. I give you tea overflowing with milk and honey. I have come to feed the hunger inside of you for God. Intention, desire, longing, all are words that express the desire for this kind of love. If you go to the center of your being and sit right down, believe me, I will be there. Trust your Grandmother God."

EMMA HOFSTEDE

Bluebird Love

Spring is the season for bird lovers to be ecstatic. Here on our porch this week we have seen the Red-Breasted Grosbeaks, the Scarlet Tanagers, Baltimore Orioles, and our friends the Pileated Woodpeckers. The Finches sit on our feeders like yellow Christmas tree lights.

Grandmother God is in her glory. She wants to do everything she can on the porch so she won't miss a new arrival. She's like a lover in an airport waiting for her feathered friends. The one bird that really gets us excited is the Indigo Bunting. You are just lucky if you get a glimpse. This bird is like a small piece of God wrapped in blue feathers. Really though, there is no blue like the flash you see when the bluebird lifts up off the grass.

The other morning, Grandmother God and I were up early having a cup of jasmine tea. We could hear the Wren singing somewhere in the woods. We both agreed that this is about as good as it gets. It has a love song with a long lilting trill that calls to his mate.

Being with her as we watch the birds is like sitting on the rim of heaven. She doesn't say anything, but she is mighty happy that spring has finally decided to come and stay.

Don't forget she loves you so much. She will sit up close, put her arm around you, and you will feel pure Bluebird Love.

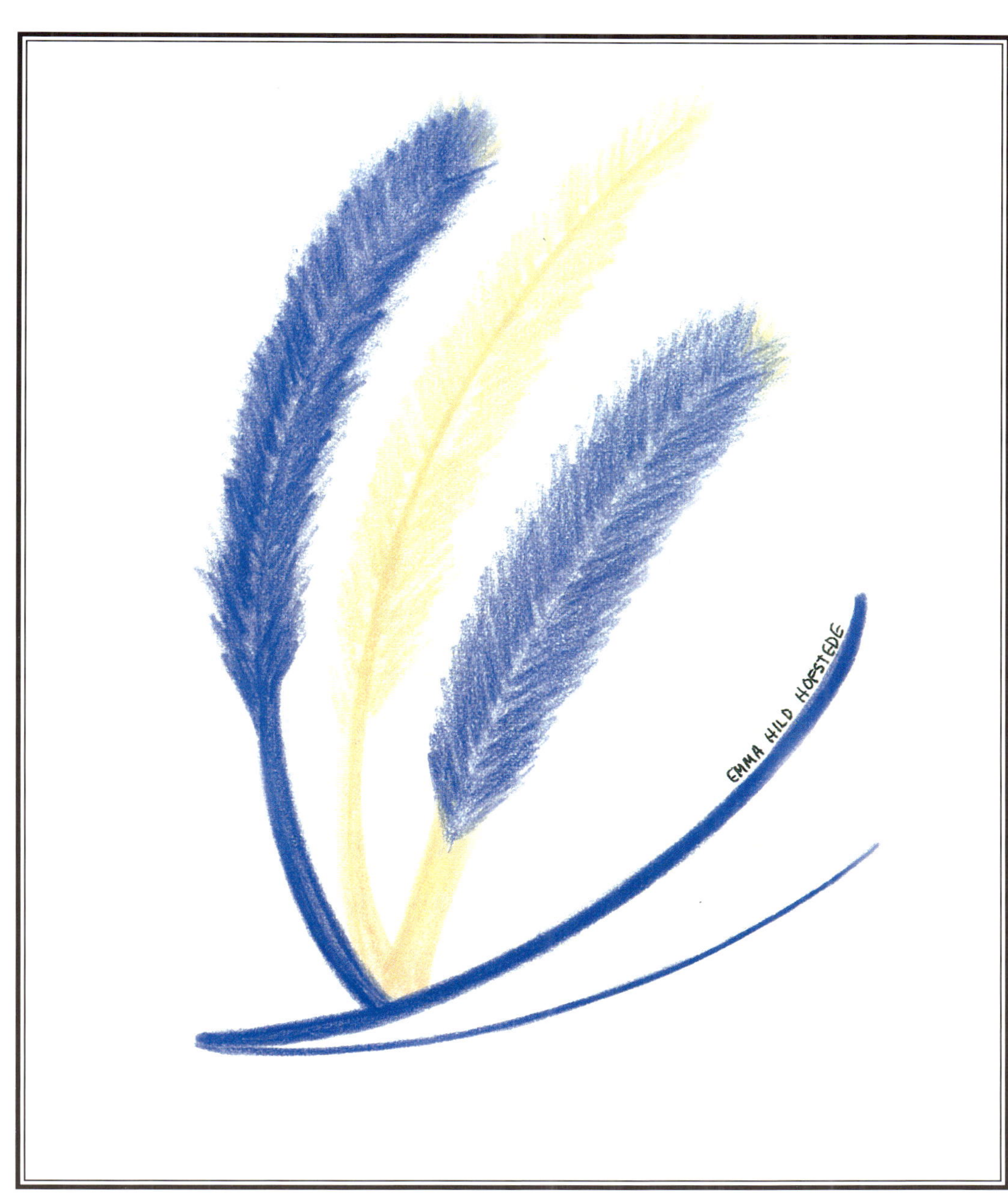

EMMA HILD HOFSTEDE

Sweeter Than Honey

Today Grandmother God and I were reading about God's precepts in Psalm 19. We don't often think of laws as sweet, but in this Psalm they are called sensuously luscious, objects of desire and a source of sweetness. The honey comes from the sweetest imaginable honeys.

> "More desired than gold,
> than abundant fine gold,
> and sweeter than honey,
> quintessence of bees."

You know how Grandmother God is really into sweetness. She loves the line from Scripture, "Taste and see that the Lord is sweet." We also know how she has a bent for making delicious desserts, like peach pie and chocolate chip cookies. She says those are just a faint taste of the sweetness of God.

She wants you to know that she shares her sweetness like water flowing over Niagara Falls. When you are feeling the need for restoration of any kind, just sit right down with her, and she will soothe your hurts.

Really these sweet Psalm words are about keeping the laws of God, but Grandmother God favors the comforting aspect of honey. She knows how hard life is here on this planet. She has come to grace us with her presence, support us in any way she can, and give us the sweetest love.

Think about that as you go about your day, the sweetness of an unimaginable number of bees is yours for the asking.

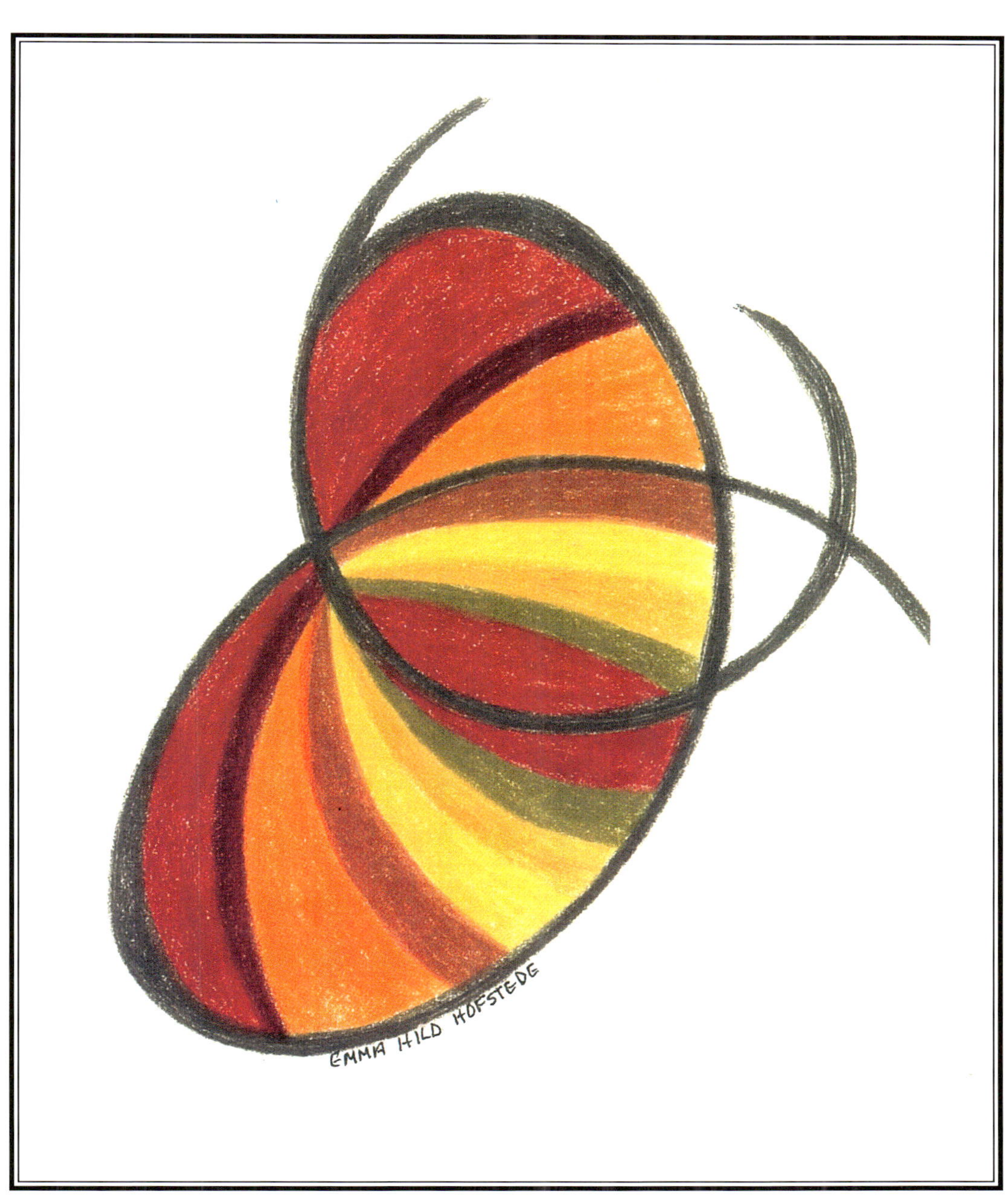

EMMA HILD HOFSTEDE

A Brilliant Light Shining from Within

Wouldn't it be nice to see this light?

Psalm 119:
"The portal of your words sends forth light."

The footnote refers to the light as, "a brilliant light shining forth from within."

Grandmother God said, "Honey, that is you, your spirit and body are one. You give off a brilliant light. It is hard for people to see it in each other. Remember the story when Thomas Merton went into Lexington, Kentucky, he said how wonderful it would be if people could only see how they shine. I have always loved those words. If we could see this brilliant light, how differently we would treat each other and ourselves.

"That is why I have come, to help everyone know about the light glowing within each of you. In the East they greet each other with the word, Namaste. It is often translated to mean the holy in me greets the holy in you. Oh, Honey, we are getting closer and closer to the glorious reality of who each and every one of you are.

"I come baking pies, watching birds, planting flowers, and enjoying life with you. I am teaching you to look, to really look and see. Everything glows with this radiance, the glory of God within.

"Start by living from that deep glowing presence in your center. Spend time there. Remember this place during your day. When you live from there, life changes."

Grandmother Comfort

When it comes to compassion, Grandmother God has it in spades. She knows when someone is having a hard time. The thing about her is that she won't be the first to mention what it is she is noticing. She waits until you say you want to talk. She is with me so much that it is even harder for her to wait, but she does.

After many tears, I asked her if she would help with all the grief that is coming out of me. She said, "Honey, sit down. I will make us some tea and we'll talk." She bustled around the kitchen getting her tea things ready, and I noticed she put a few of my favorite chocolate chip cookies on a plate. We took our tea and went to sit on the sun porch. The reason I am sharing this with you is so you will know how respectful she is. She says it's like dancing, she doesn't lead, she follows, all the while holding you close. Her loving energy just seeps into your whole being.

When someone you love is going through a life and death struggle, like my husband, you have an inner strength that sustains you. It is often called grace, and it is a pure gift. When the crisis seems to be over, your feelings come pouring out. Just any gesture of kindness tends to melt the barrier you needed to get through the crisis. Grandmother God knows this and she is like a safety net there for you. She says, "Let the tears flow. They will nourish the earth and soften the pain of all the others suffering fear and loss."

We sat on the porch and I cried and she held me. There are really no words for this kind of loved pain. I am telling you, go to her when you need comfort. She is there and waiting. What is so special about her? Her love comes with her delicious cookies and hot tea.

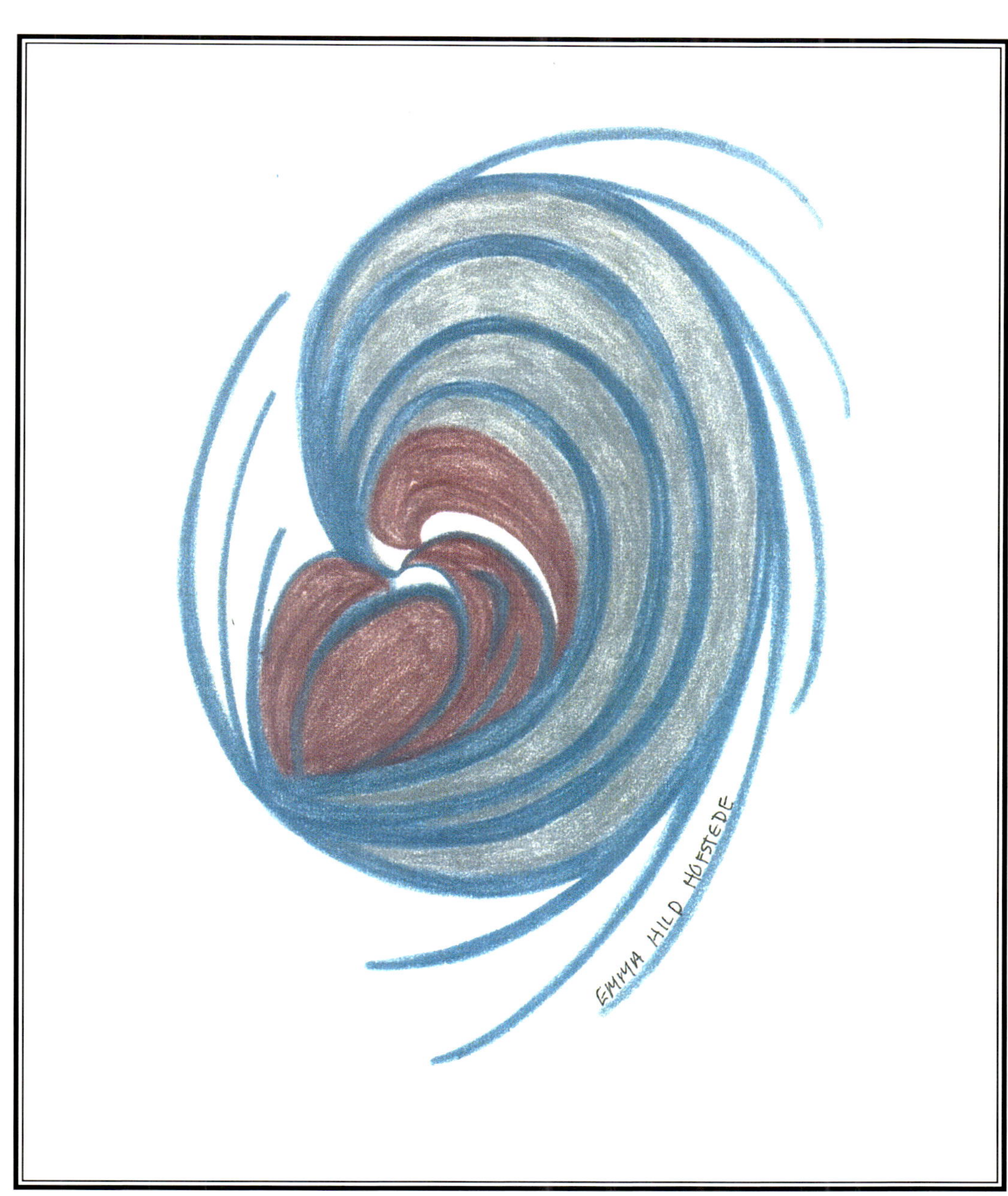
EMMA HILD HOFSTEDE

Stay Close

When Grandmother God and I were at a farm, we met a woman who was there to take care of her horses. She had a dog in her car, and when she let it out, she said, "Stay close."

The real story behind those words is that one time Momma Cat, who lives on this farm, was under the pine tree near the electric fence. The dog got shocked at the same time that the cat came out from under the tree. The dog associated the shock with the cat. Now every time she sees Momma Cat, she runs next to her owner, and that is the wisdom of those words, "Stay Close."

We loved that story. Grandmother God said that it doesn't matter if our fears are based on a real threat or not. If we associate anything with something that will hurt us, she wants us to hear those words, 'Stay Close." She will be there and we can stay close to her. She doesn't change what is happening, but she sure offers a place of refuge when we need it.

She knows that living on earth is not easy. So many things that happen here are beyond our power to change.

Grandmother God wanted us to remember those words to help us when we are scared.

Remember, "Stay Close."

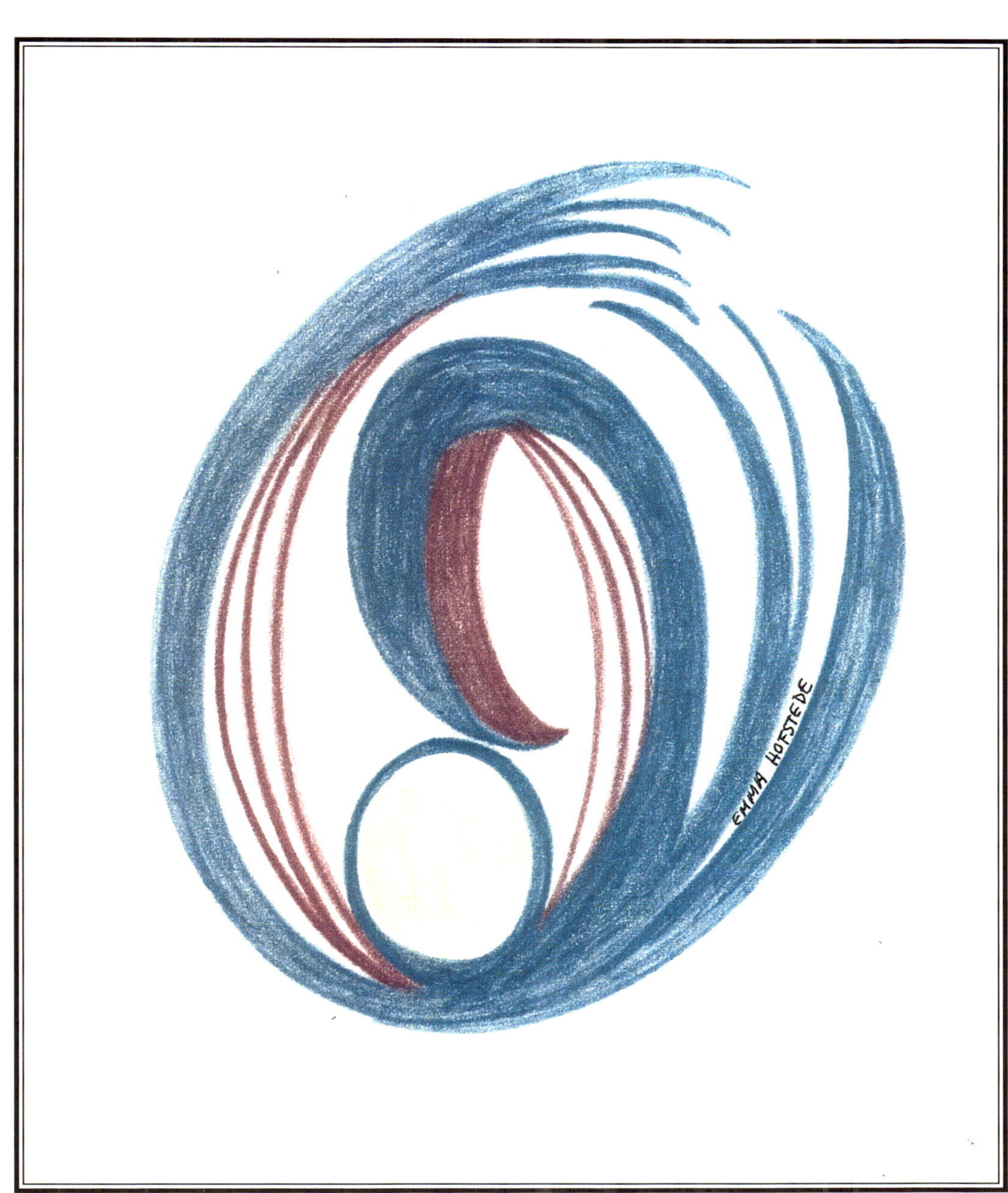

EMMA HOFSTEDE

The Love of Gardening

In the fall, flower catalogues start arriving at our house. Grandmother God puts them in a stack by her chair and looks them over and over each evening.

She is a very discerning gardener. She is looking for flowers that will bloom all season long. She has this down to a science. Creating beauty is one of her passions. If she has just a few minutes, she is out in the garden doing something important. I love being around her when spring arrives.

One thing is for sure, you almost have to make an appointment with her to have a chat. She would rather be gardening this time of year than doing almost anything else. Sometimes I just go sit out there and watch her and take in all the fragrance of the spring blossoms.

It isn't surprising that she loves gardening so much. Making a beautiful place for others to enjoy makes her so happy. Sometimes she sings when she is planting or weeding. She is so much in the moment; I bet she is in touch with God. Wait, she is God! You can see why I love being with her. She just rubs off on me in such a way that I can feel her presence just clinging to me like love glue.

You never know where she will be next, but right now she is watching that snow melt, and the temperature rise. Pretty soon she will be out there whistling and singing. She has a pretty cool gardening hat too.

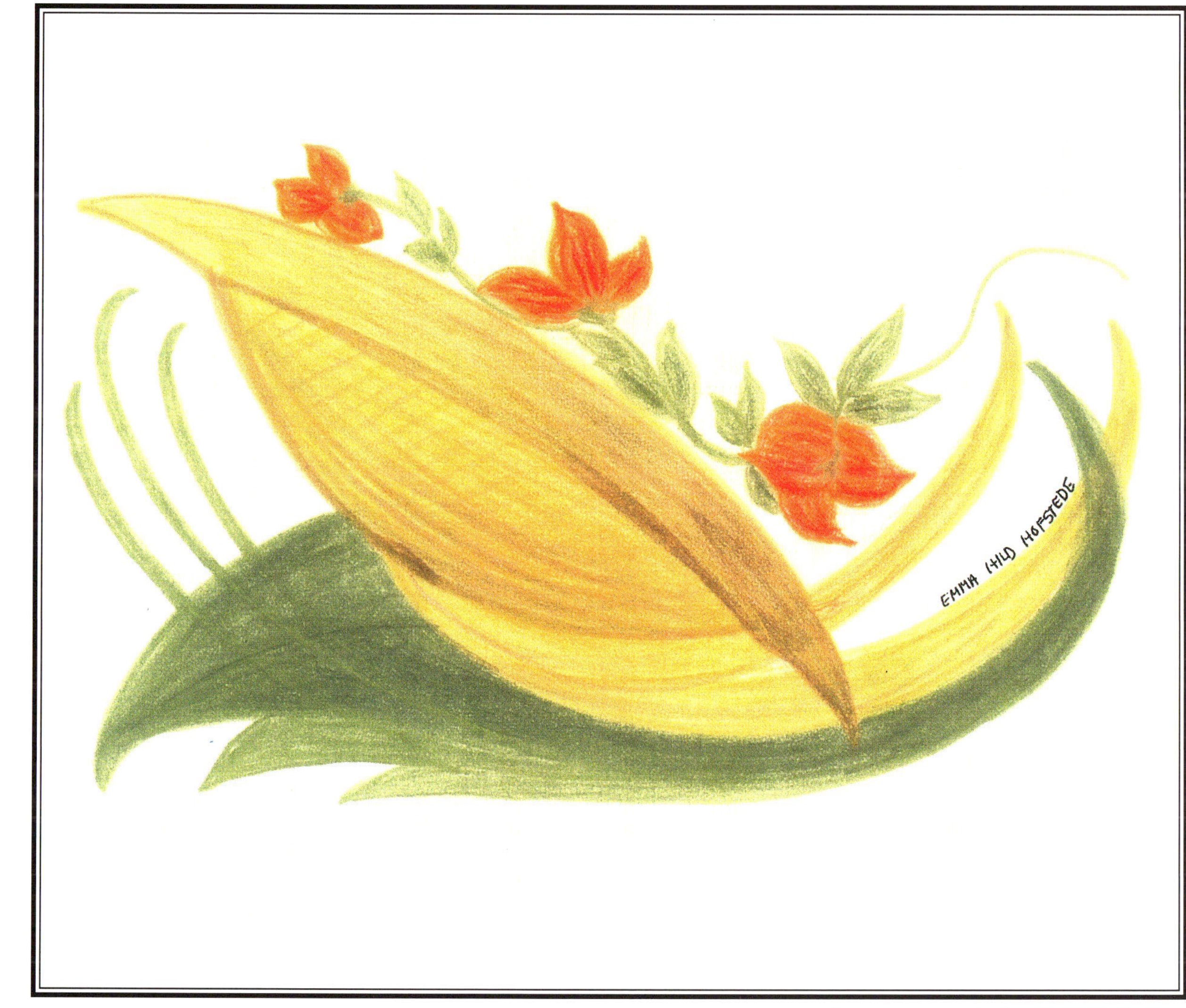

EMMA CHILD HOFSTEDE

Cloud Carnival

Today is a beautiful 70-degree day. The blue sky is carrying white fluffy clouds in its arms. Grandmother God loves clouds almost more than anything else in nature. I was surprised she said that, because I always thought that clouds and trees were some of God's best ideas. She stuck to clouds.

They are stacked up like pillows on a big blue-sky bed, just waiting to carry us aloft into God's billowy arms. Can't you just imagine lying back into all that white softness and sailing across the sky with the wind? You can look around and see all the other clouds drifting along beside you. Maybe an angel is tucked inside one of them.

Grandmother God thought she'd have her own cloud carnival for her friends. She would have cloud rides, shooting star jumps, and rainbow sliding. She is getting pretty excited about this. In line with the cloud theme, she is thinking cotton candy, strawberry ice cream, and lemonade served cloud-side. Sometimes I think she has just about the best imagination of anyone.

The real point is that Grandmother God will hold you close, wrapped in a blanket as soft as a cloud. In her arms, love can seep into every cell of your body. She loves you so much, and offers love and cloud comfort to you.

This talk is pure whimsy on Grandmother God's part, but that is what is so lovable about her. Today the beauty of clouds enraptures her, tomorrow who knows!

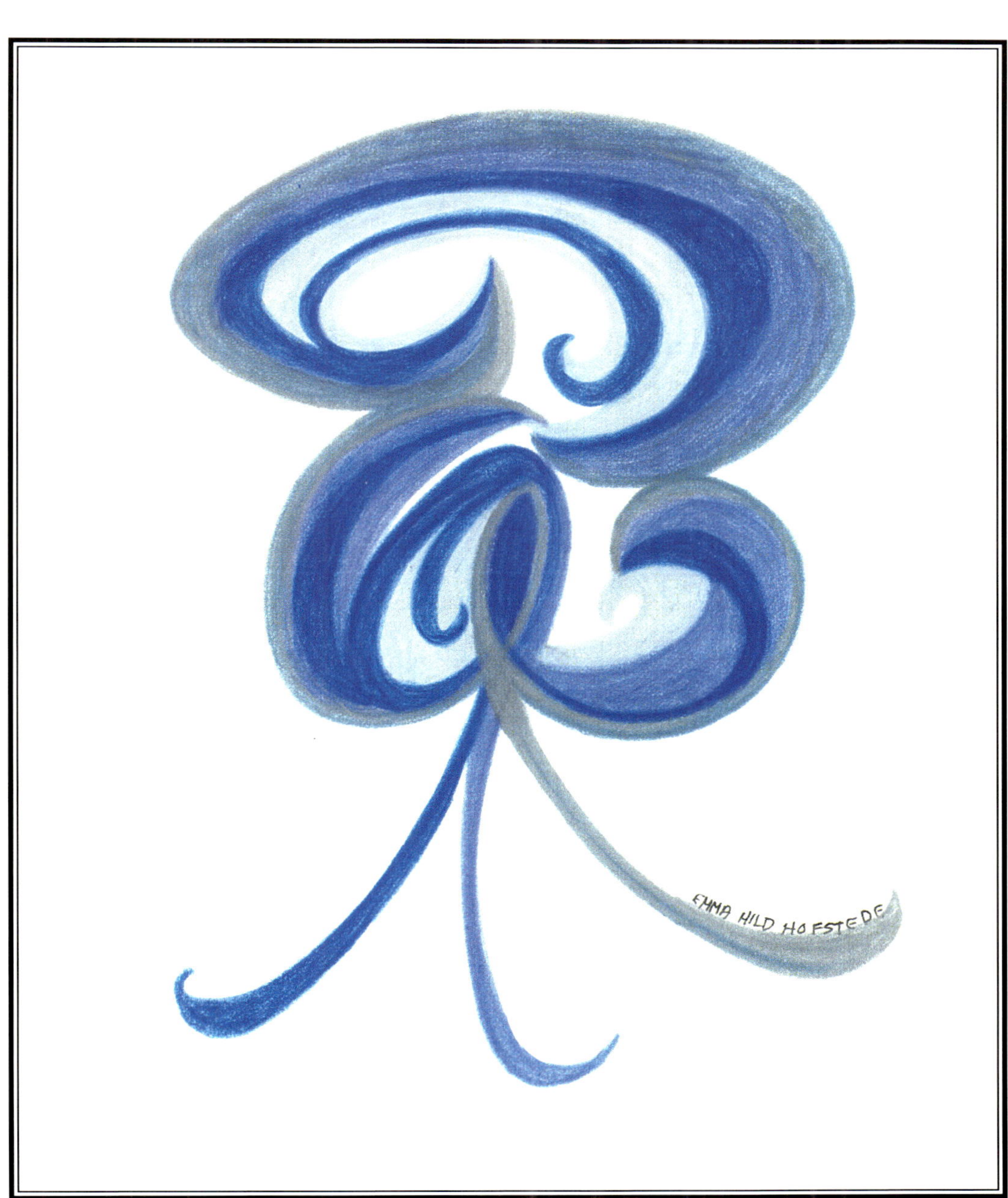
EMMA HILD HOFSTEDE

The Power of Love

We are up at our cabin waiting for a rainstorm to move down the lake. It is not like in the city when you can actually see it approach. This is how it is when it comes to hearing sad news, I don't know which is better, sudden awareness, or to be able to see it coming.

We received some pretty frightening news about a friend of ours. I asked Grandmother God how does a human being bear the unbearable? She was not quick in answering this question. She came over and sat next to me and put her arm around me and did not say anything. We both just sat there in the quiet listening to the rain, and holding one another. I guess she pretty much answered the question. We have each other.

I asked her how you handle the feelings that whirl around inside you scaring you to death, feelings that no human being should have to deal with, yet there they are right in the middle of your life. Again Grandmother God did not say anything, she just continued to hold me close and I realized then that there are no words for this kind of pain.

She started to sing a song. Her voice was beautiful, soft and gentle like the sound of the falling rain. It calmed us both.

It is when things are hard that family and friends help. They come and gather around and form an energy field that enables everyone to at least cope. Grandmother God agreed with me and said when we call on her she will add her energy to strengthen the magnificent power of human love.

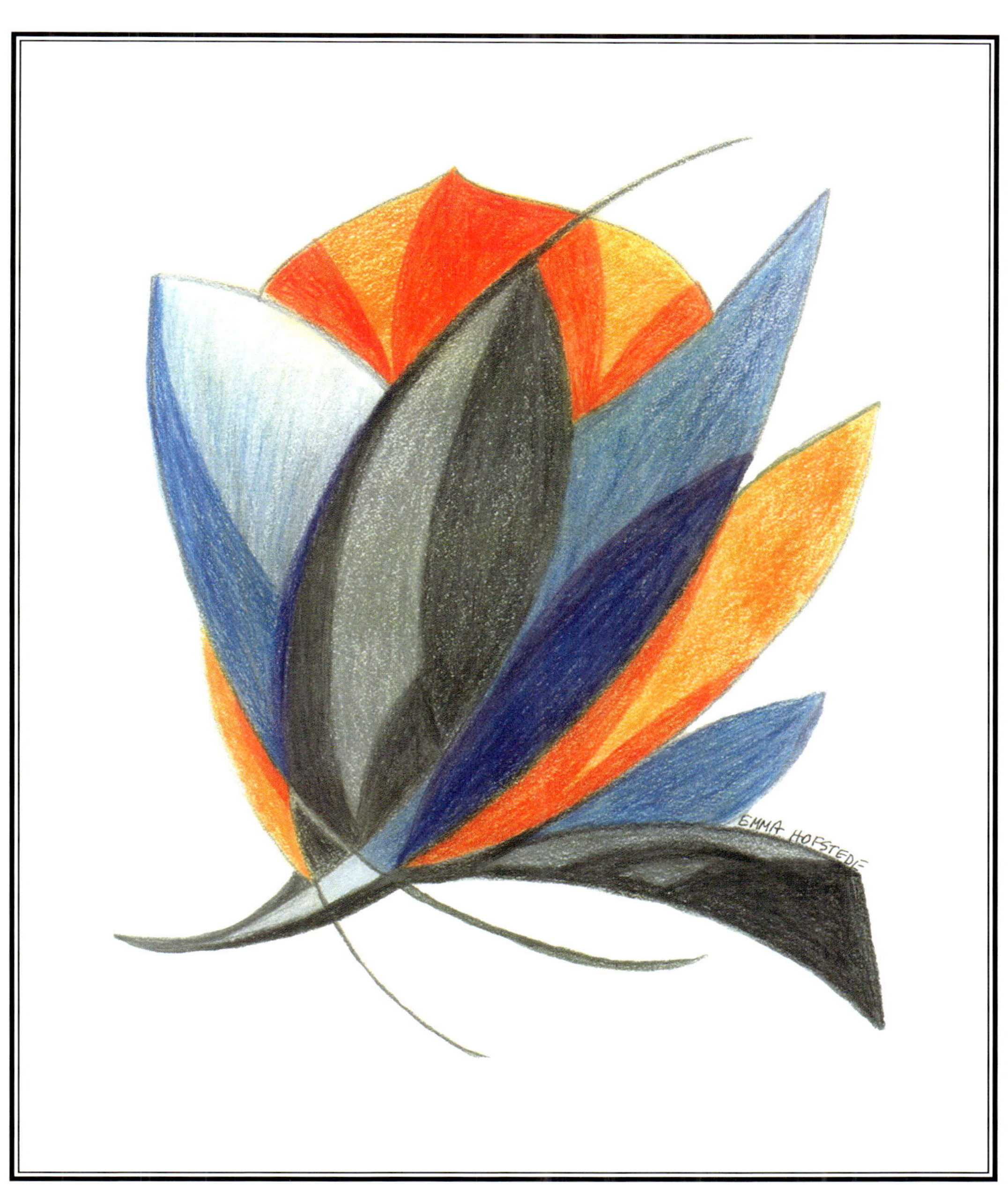
EMMA HOFSTEDE

Streams of Delight

This morning in Psalm 36, God has us drink from streams of delight, and is imagined as a fountain of light.

> "They take their fill from the fare of your house
> and from Your stream of delight You give them
> drink. For with You is the fountain of light.
> In Your light we shall see light."

Drinking from streams of light, wrapped in light, how much closer can God get to us? Those are some pretty snappy images for you to carry with you today.

Grandmother God is really serious about living from our center. It is impossible not to love if you are sitting in the source of love.

Grandmother God says that when you feel unease, you have wandered from that deep loving place inside, and you are sitting smack dab in the middle of your ego. You get tossed around trying to sort out what everyone is saying and doing. When you sit with Grandmother God in your center, you are breathing the air of peace, love, and joy.

Remember when you are with her, she serves goodies. Her company is the best part, but her pies and cookies sure add to the delight of being together.

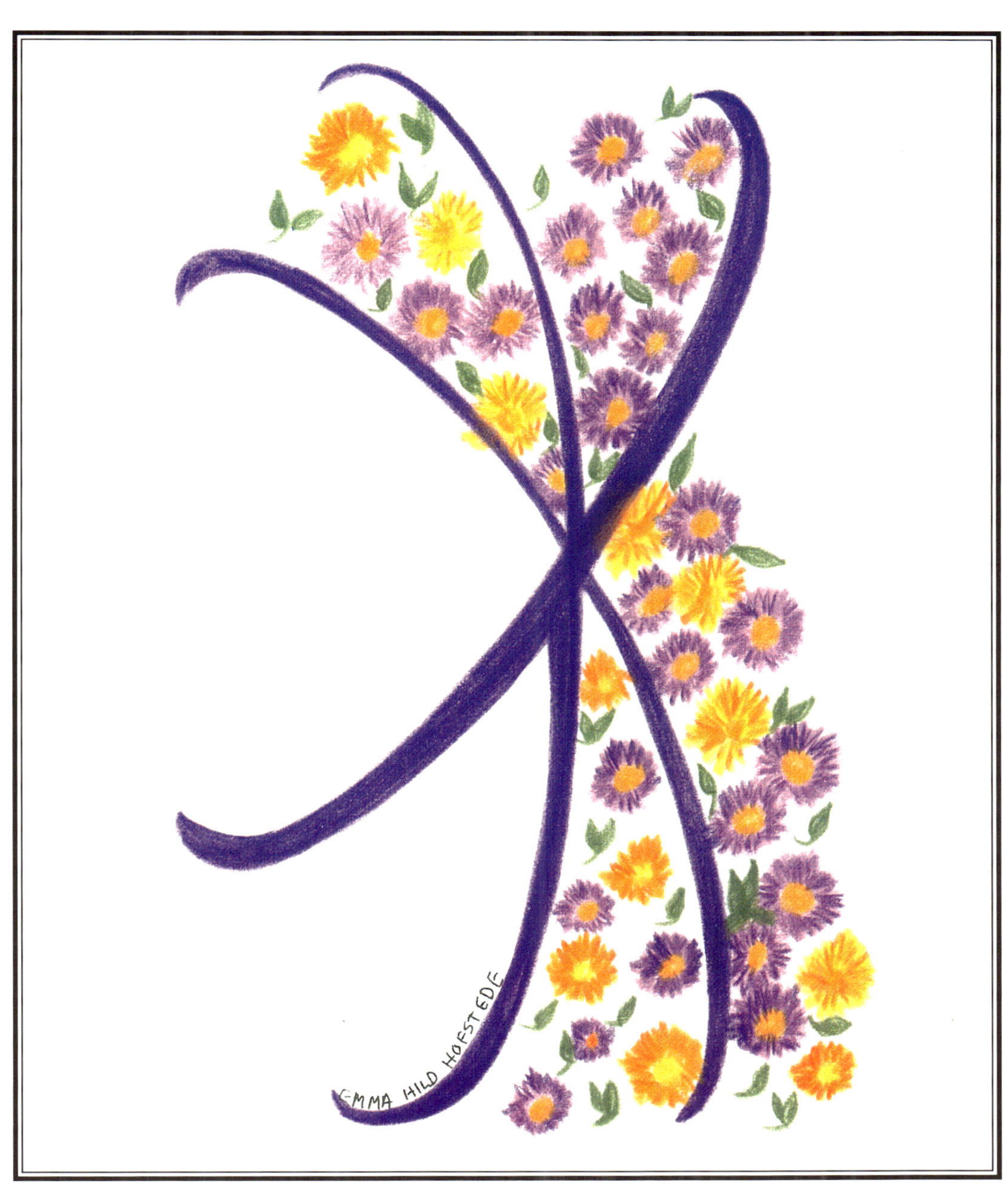

EMMA HILD HOFSTEDE

Sunrise Surprise

Our good friend Joe died yesterday. He was 95. During all of his retired years Joe lived on our lake. Last night I asked God for a sign that he was all right. I will always have that question in my mind. Where do people go when they die?

I woke up this morning at 5:00 A.M., something that is unusual for me. I looked out the window and it was as if someone had splashed brilliant reds, oranges and yellows across the sky and then took a bucket of color and filled the lake so it looked like the sky and the water were one. I knew that it was Joe saying, "I'm fine, look and see the beauty of my lake."

Grandmother God just smiled when I told her about it. She knows how hard death is for us. Our loved ones just disappear. It is so hard to adjust to this. You can still hear the sound of their voices, and see their faces. You can hardly believe that you won't see them again. All your feelings about them return and seem to light up your movie screen inside so in this way they are still with you.

Grandmother God speaks words of comfort whenever she can. "Honey," she said, "He had a wonderful life, so many years, and so many fish. We will honor him and love him always. Human beings are so tender and precious to me. The way you feel for each other touches my heart."

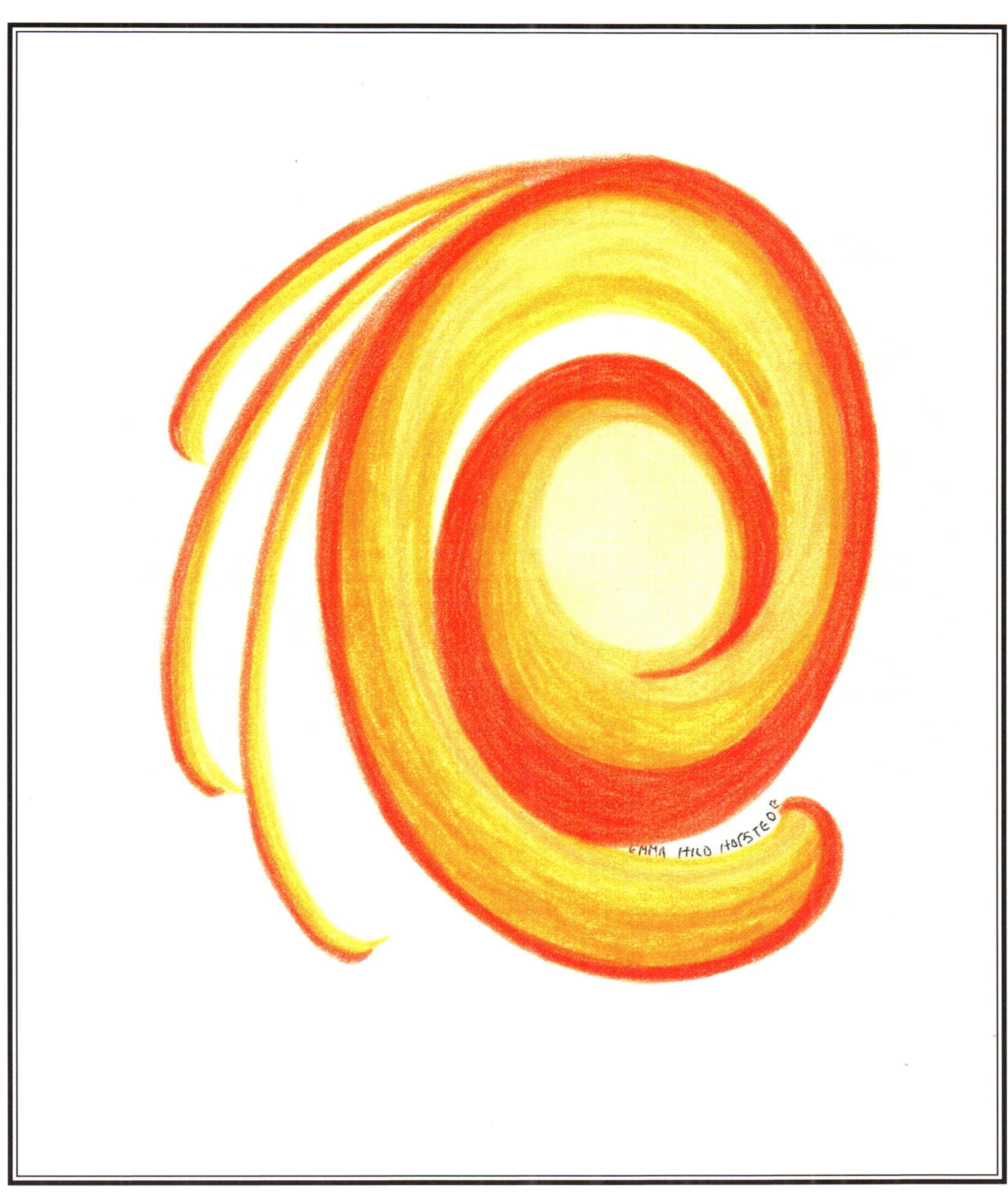

EMMA HILD HOFSTEDE

Comfy Love

Grandmother God is in the mood to sit down and have a chat.

She has lots of things she likes to do, but talking with her friends is her favorite. She has made tea and apricot scones. She prefers sitting in front of the fire when it is cold out. Yesterday we had a snowstorm, and the trees look like they are in a fairyland covered with a thick layer of pure white snow.

When Grandmother God has something on her mind, she comes right to the point, that is, after the tea is poured. She says right out that she lives inside each one of us and that we are a unique expression of how she loves.

Hearing these words makes you just want to lean back into her precious warm presence and disappear. Actually that is what happens, and you may even hear her heartbeat.

Really living with the power of this love could change the world. Imagine if we all did that!

I love Grandmother God. She is so easy to be with, no airs on her part, just plain comfy love.

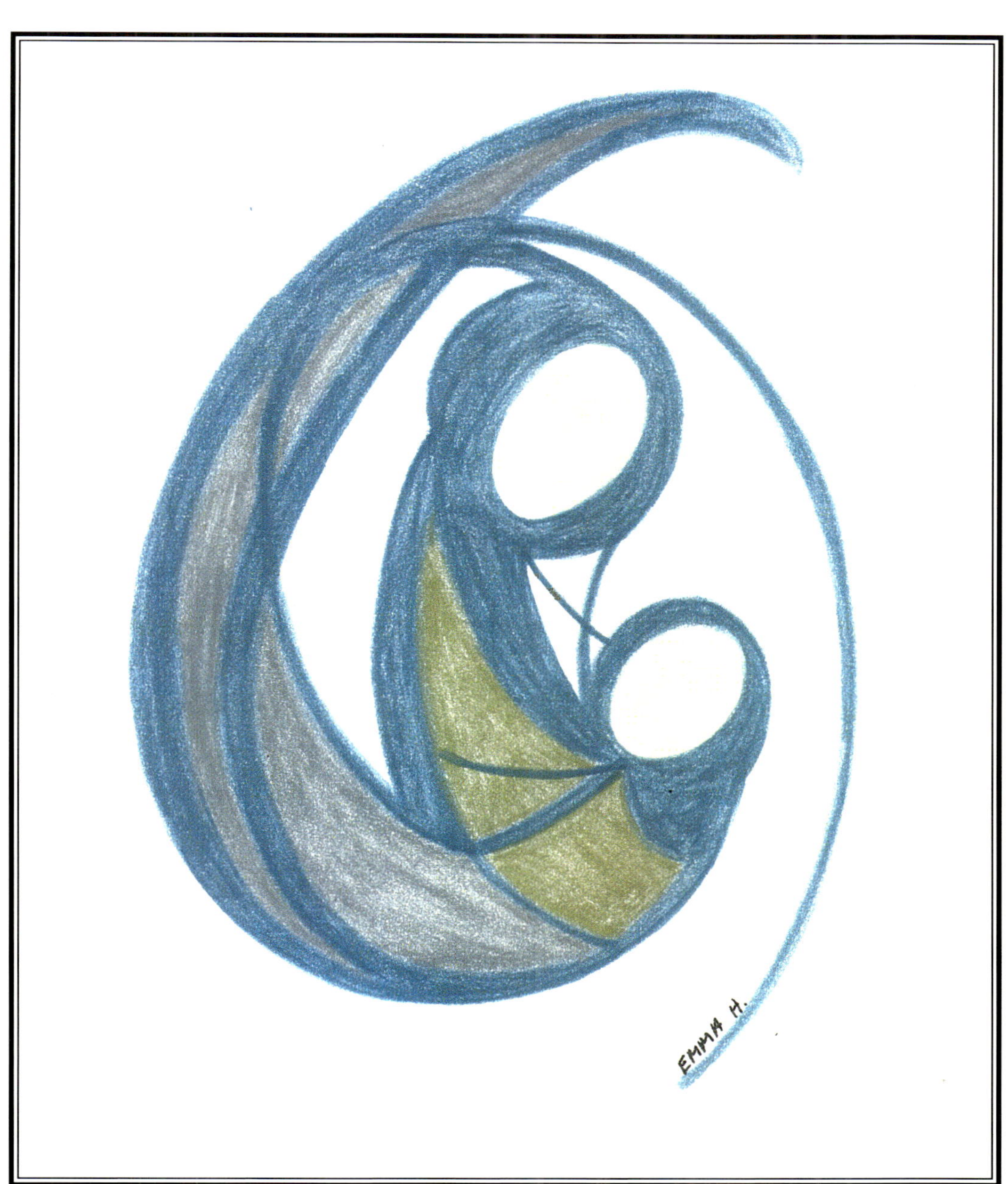

Grandmother God's Arrival

Don't you wonder who the lucky ones are who get to actually see those little green buds pop out on the trees? It's like you turn your head for a split second, and there they are! I can almost hear them sing out, "Surprise!" Honestly, even Grandmother God missed it this spring.

I never did tell you how she came into my life. One day I was reading in my living room, and I turned my head, and there she was. A beautiful radiant woman was sitting on my flowered sofa in a flowered dress. She just appeared. She had such a look of love on her face that I am surprised that I didn't melt into my own chair. I said, "Who are you, and how did you get in here?" She just smiled and held out her hand and I was just like the amazed Apostles who dropped their nets and walked off with Jesus. Ever since that day I have been her friend and scribe.

She told me she had come to fill to overflowing everyone's hearts with love. She wanted us to experience what God is really like. This time and place was her choice. She bakes pies, makes tea, dances, plants flowers, and enjoys some television shows, like American Idol. She is always available for you. She lives in your heart.

I loved her immediately. She is like being with the Sun, Moon, Stars, and the whole Cosmos put together. Along with all that dazzle, you feel so loved that your heart twizzles and spins, and there you sit, like a big red juicy tomato filled with love.

Remember, she loves you so much, and invites you to call on her any time of the day or night. She will be with you and you might just get lucky and get some of her warm blueberry pie and jasmine tea.

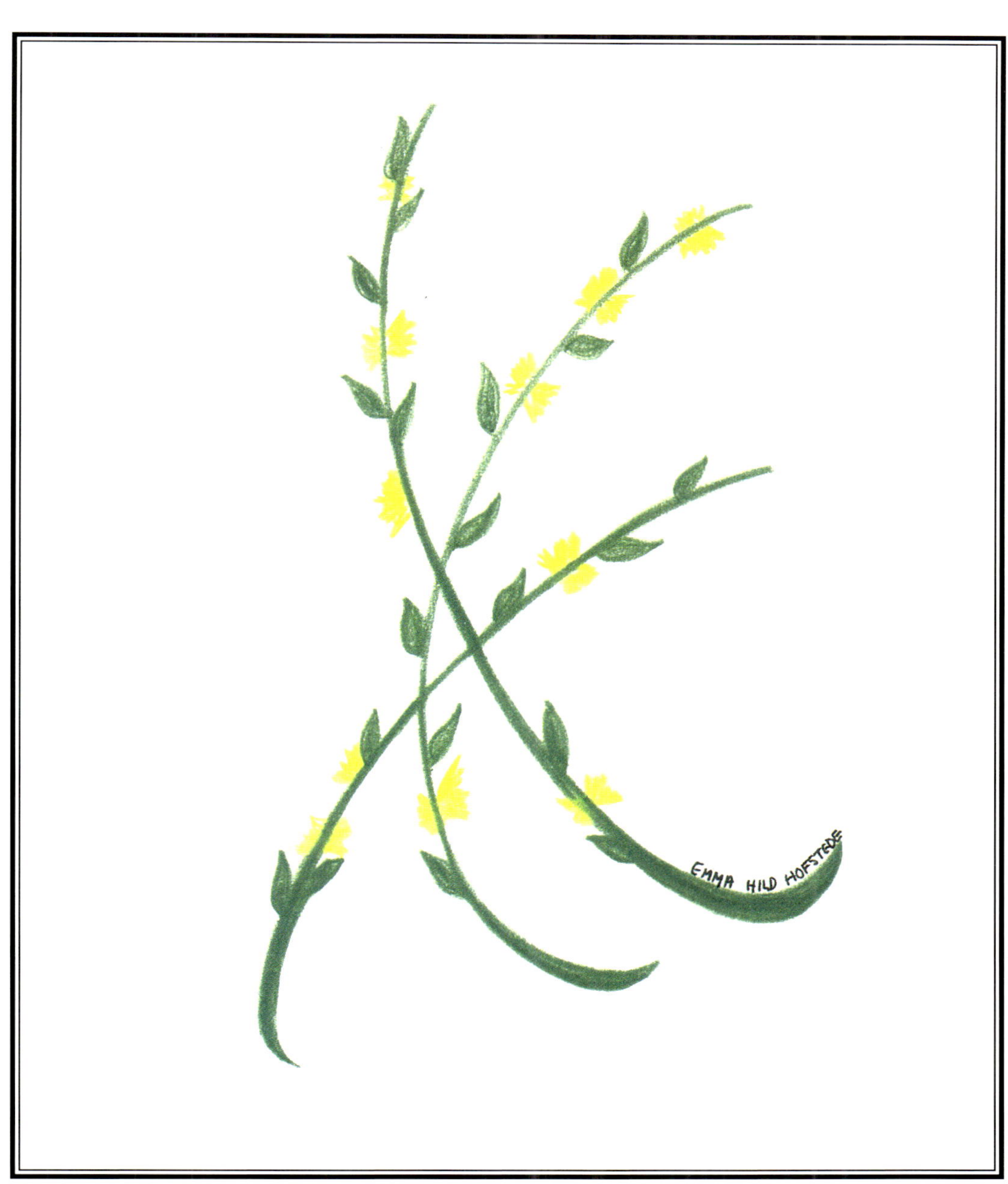

EMMA HILD HOFSTEDE

Grandmother God and Suffering

Grandmother God knows how much we want to be able to be present for our friends when they need support. She is the queen of supporters. Sometimes she just sits quietly next to you and holds your hand, and other times she has words of comfort. She instinctively knows what you need. Her presence is like a warm summer breeze filled with the smells of prairie flowers and sun.

There are some feelings that are inconsolable. It seems we all encounter them at various times in our lives. Grandmother God knows all about them. She doesn't have any answers; she just enters your heart with a love that fills every nook and cranny. When you breathe, she wafts sweetness into your being to console you from the inside. Nothing else seems to quiet the fear quite like her presence.

I asked her why life was so hard sometimes. She just looked at me and said, "Honey, it just is." She said what we call grace is actually her presence, and it strengthens you to get through the storms. You can't explain how you did get through some impossible situations. She said, "Yes, that's it. You do, and when you look back you are surprised at what you were able to do.

"Oh, dear one, just know that what people offer each other in the way of comfort and affection is part of God's plan. You are co-comforters with me. No answer is adequate because there is no answer. I stick to that. I am Grandmother God, and I do not try to explain suffering.

"Know that when you call on me, I am there. I am there all the time, but calling makes me hurry all the more, and deepens the possibility of your feeling my presence sooner.

"Tell all my dear ones to trust and love, and hold my hand."

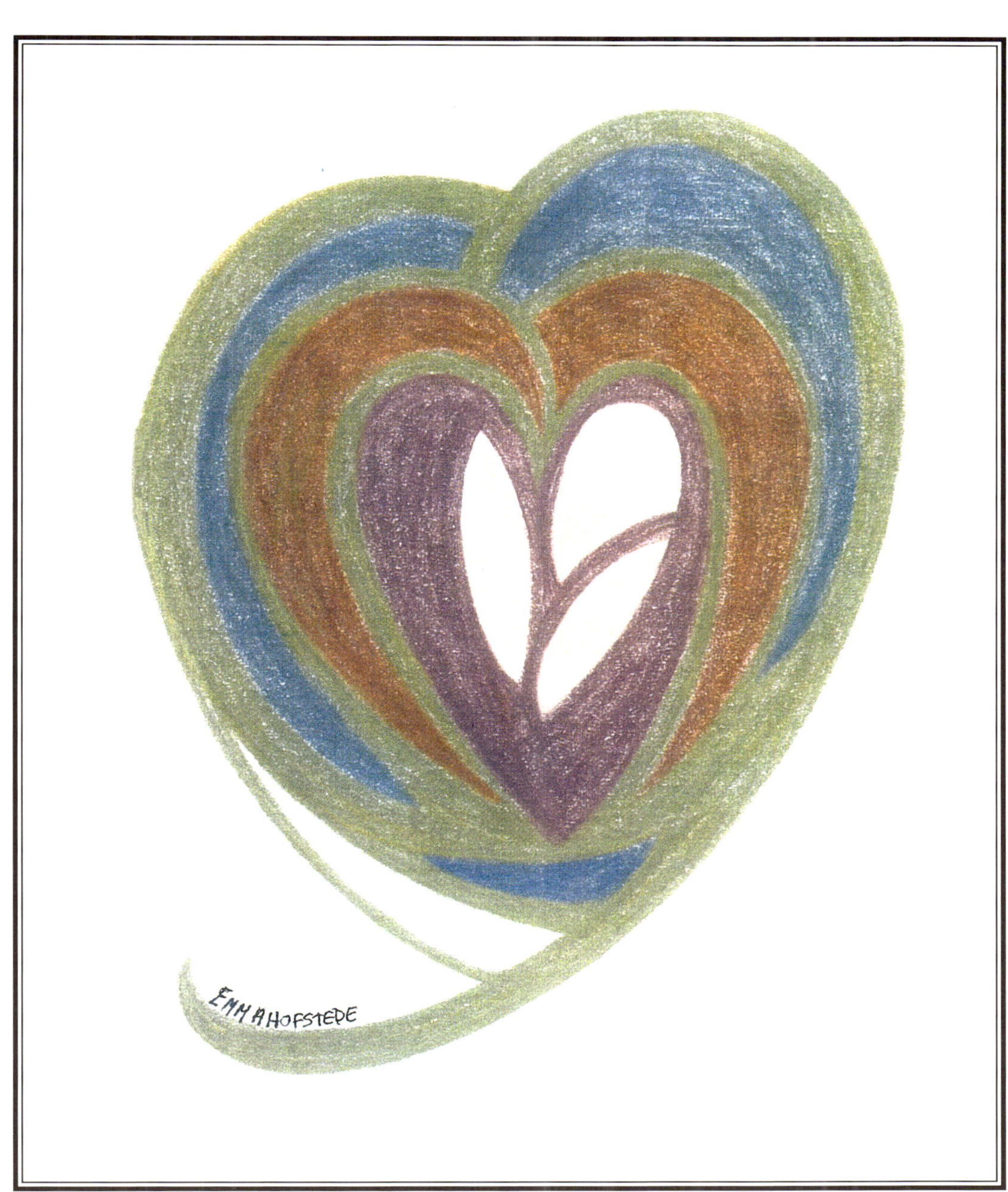

EMMA HOFSTEDE

Grandmother God Goes Drumming

One thing I love about Grandmother God is that she will try anything once. Her friends invited her to go drumming. I told her she could use my drum and off we went.

When people started to arrive she sat with a look of utter amazement at the variety of their drums. There was a lot of warming up like an orchestra getting ready to perform. It created a feeling of anticipation.

A man who sat across the aisle from us had a huge drum almost four times the size of a kettledrum. It had a deep resonance. He told us it was from Pakistan. Sitting next to him was a man with a didgeridoo. It is a five or six foot long hollowed out gourd painted a shiny eggplant purple. It made such a deep sound you could feel the vibration within you.

The atmosphere of the room was enhanced with candlelight. When the drumming began, the Shaman walked around and signaled a specific beat that each section was to follow. When all of the different sounds came together the effect was awesome.

Grandmother God was drumming along with everyone else and had a look on her face like she had left the earth. She really loved the way the Shaman bobbed up and down and led the drummers into this amazing music.

When we were driving home, I asked her if she enjoyed the evening. She said, "Yes, but I was hoping for an out-of-body experience." I just kept driving. Imagine her wanting that. She is something isn't she!

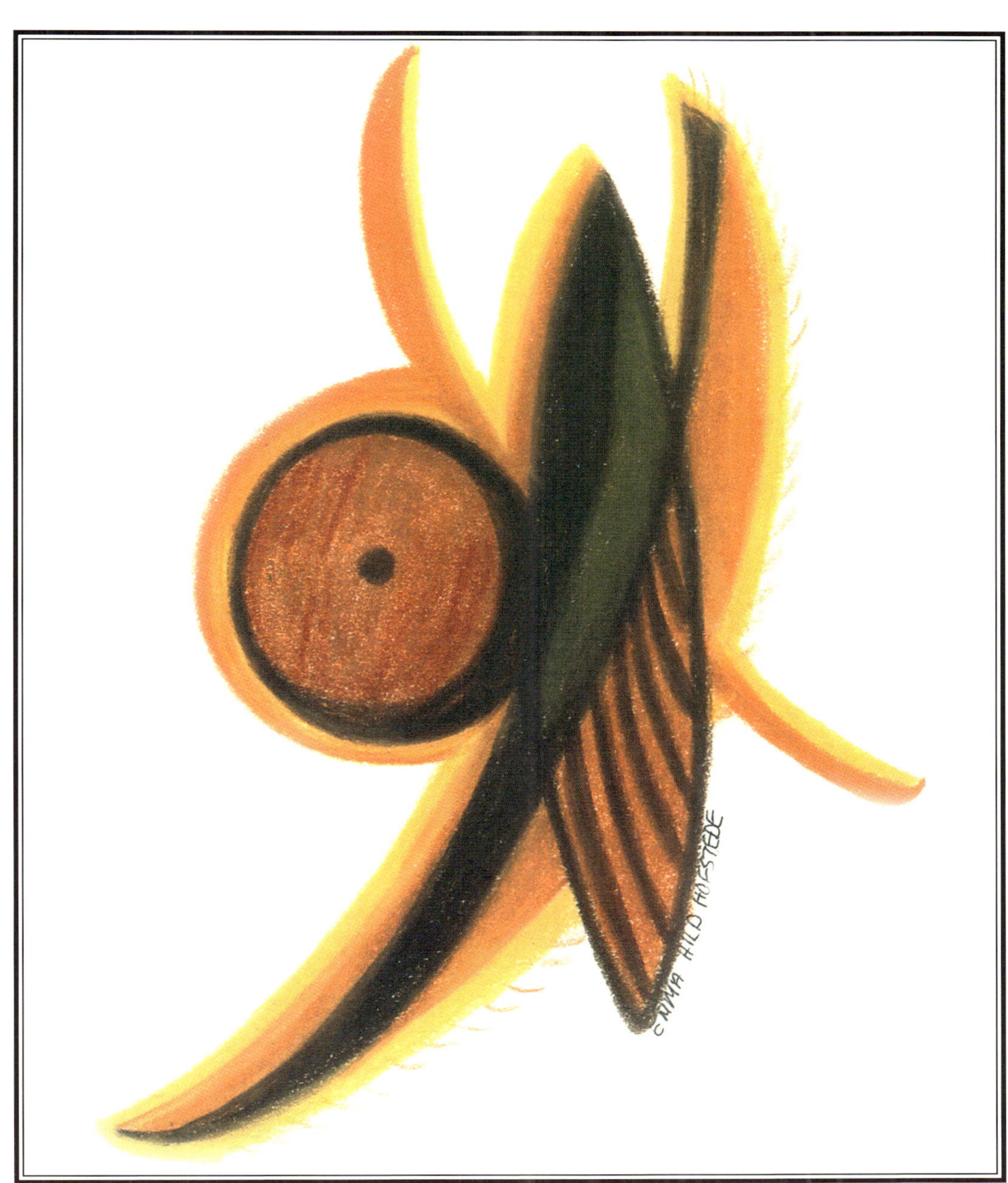

Honey from the Rock

"And I would feed him the finest wheat, and from the rock I would sate him with honey." Psalm 81

Grandmother God loves those words. She shows her love by nourishing us with sweetness. This is not like sugar, but the essence from millions of flowers. She knows when honey is right. Grandmother God bakes peach and blueberry pies, chocolate chip cookies and occasionally scones. In our world these pastries are the honey from the rock. In Scripture it says, "Taste and see that God is sweet." It is this kind of sweetness Grandmother God is talking about.

Basically she says that we are nourished by love. That is what the honey symbolizes. We just do not get enough sweetness. She knows that, and she is here to give you all you need. When you let her love you, the love flows out to others. I think it is working because she is spreading love around like sugar on donuts.

So when you are baking delicious pies and cakes, think about sprinkling lots of your love into them, and you too will be serving honey from the rock, the sweetness of God.

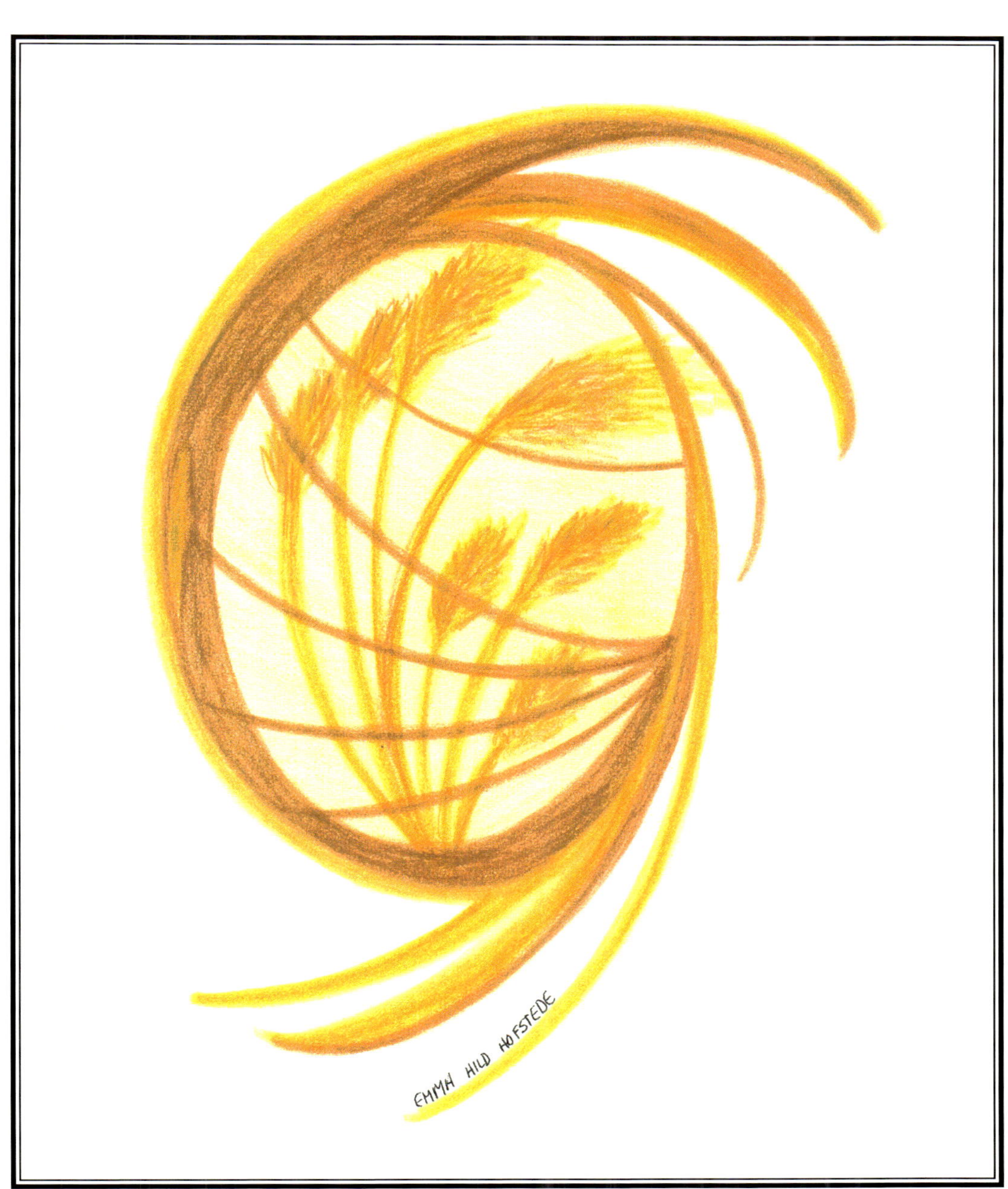
EMMA HILD HOFSTEDE

Sunday Bliss

Early in the morning when the sun is just coming up behind the woods in our back-yard, you can see a real peep show. Grandmother God and I sit and watch the sunlight slowly slide down through the trees until the leaves and the lawn are streaked with light. You can actually watch it like a slow motion film. We sit with our tea and enjoy this sweet glimpse of nature.

Today is Sunday and the day has that nice easy feeling that comes with no set plans, just living in the moment and noticing what is happening.

We are trying a new kind of jasmine tea from England. Actually we are more into the aroma than the taste. When you smell jasmine, it reminds you of the sweet smell of warm summer nights.

Grandmother God loves the fragrances of flowers and nature. We picked a big bunch of red, white and pink peonies yesterday from our back yard. Our whole living room is filled with this glorious smell. I have noticed that when we are taking a walk and Grandmother God sees a flowering tree, she puts her face right into the blossoms and feels the soft petals against her face. I love how she lets herself experience the beauty of our earth. Walking with Grandmother God on a Sunday afternoon is the best.

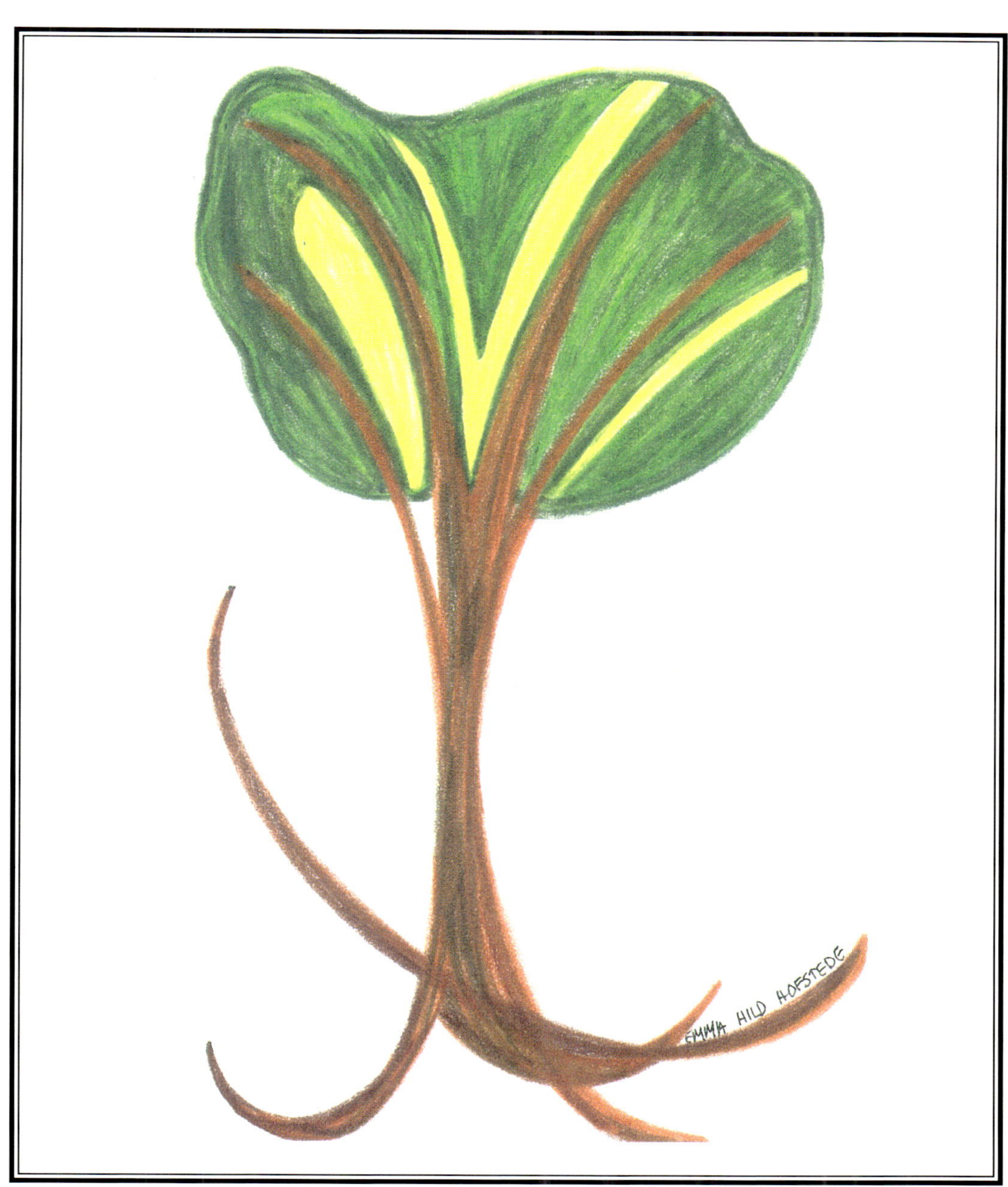

EMMA HILD HOFSTEDE

Grandmother God Is Crying

Grandmother God is crying this morning. I am right with her telling her it is all right to cry all day if she wants. I know that it doesn't seem possible that Grandmother God cries, but who knows what she carries in that great big Grandmother God heart?

I think that for so long she did not have close friends, and felt no one could see or feel her presence. I read once that God created us so she would have someone to dine with. Now if that doesn't fit Grandmother God I don't know what does. I guess I would add play with, dance with, and anything else she likes to do.

As I watch her cry, I realize she has a glorious capacity to honor her feelings, and because of that, she honors yours too. I think that is why so many people love being with her.

She likes to tell stories, and once she told me that feelings were like the colors of the rainbow. Whatever you are feeling creates a lovely arch of color to paint across the sky. I love the way she talks. Right now she is painting a broad stripe of blue, which matches her sad feelings today.

It is her capacity to feel that draws you so close to her. When she cries, her tears smell like spring rain and freshly mowed grass. Maybe she would like a few words of love from you today. Even Grandmother God likes to be comforted.

I will watch closely when she is mixing another color and ask her what feeling is rising within her. How she gets those bans so evenly arched across the sky is a secret only she knows.

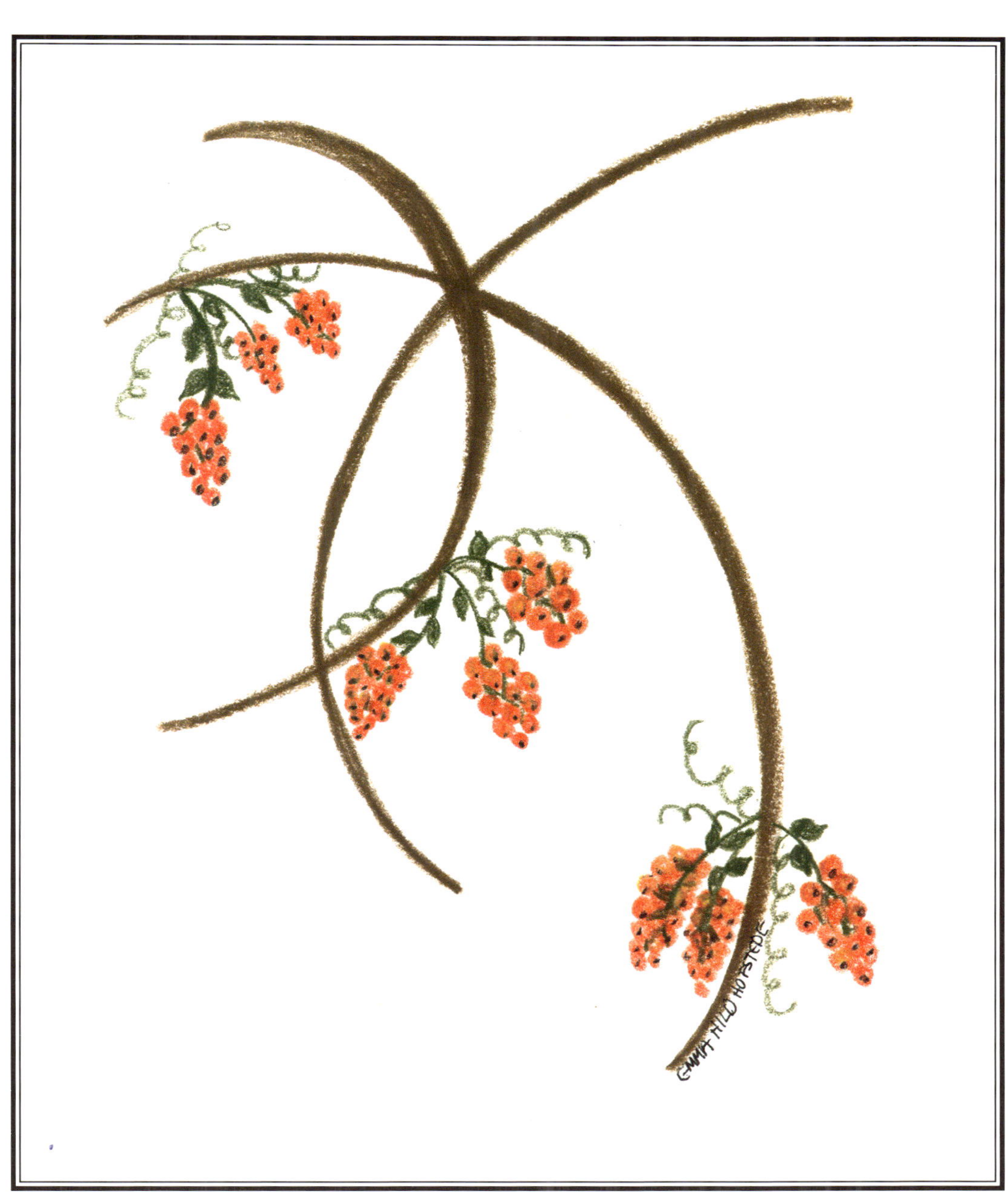
EMMA HILD HOFSTEDE

Grandmother God Goes Dancing

All day long she had itchy feet. Every once in awhile Grandmother God gets the urge to go dancing. She likes to dance in private because she doesn't want everyone wondering is this Grandmother God dancing? She does like to have a few of her friends go with her however, so consider yourself invited.

She has regular dancing clothes. She likes swirly skirts, comfy clothes and fancy shoes. Occasionally she brings brightly colored scarves that she can twirl when she spins. I tell you she can cut quite a rug.

This time we are going dancing in the woods. In the middle there is a clearing of green grass that is filled with meadow flowers. We bring our own music, or sometimes just listen to the music of the forest. I am sure she also has some special tune in her head, because she starts swirling and turning even before we get there.

I love to watch her dance. She is not too young, but you would never know it if you saw her move. She doesn't really care what others think because she just loves to dance. It is all in the way she moves her arms and legs. The scarves help to give that swaying gossamer feeling.

One time when I was watching her, she came over to me and grabbed me by the hand and said, "Come on Hon, let's dance." I was nervous because after all she is Grandmother God. Never mind worrying, she just took the lead and off we went dancing around the trees and hopping over stumps. WOW! What a wonderful time we had. And, whenever you get that dancing feeling, she'll be right there with you.

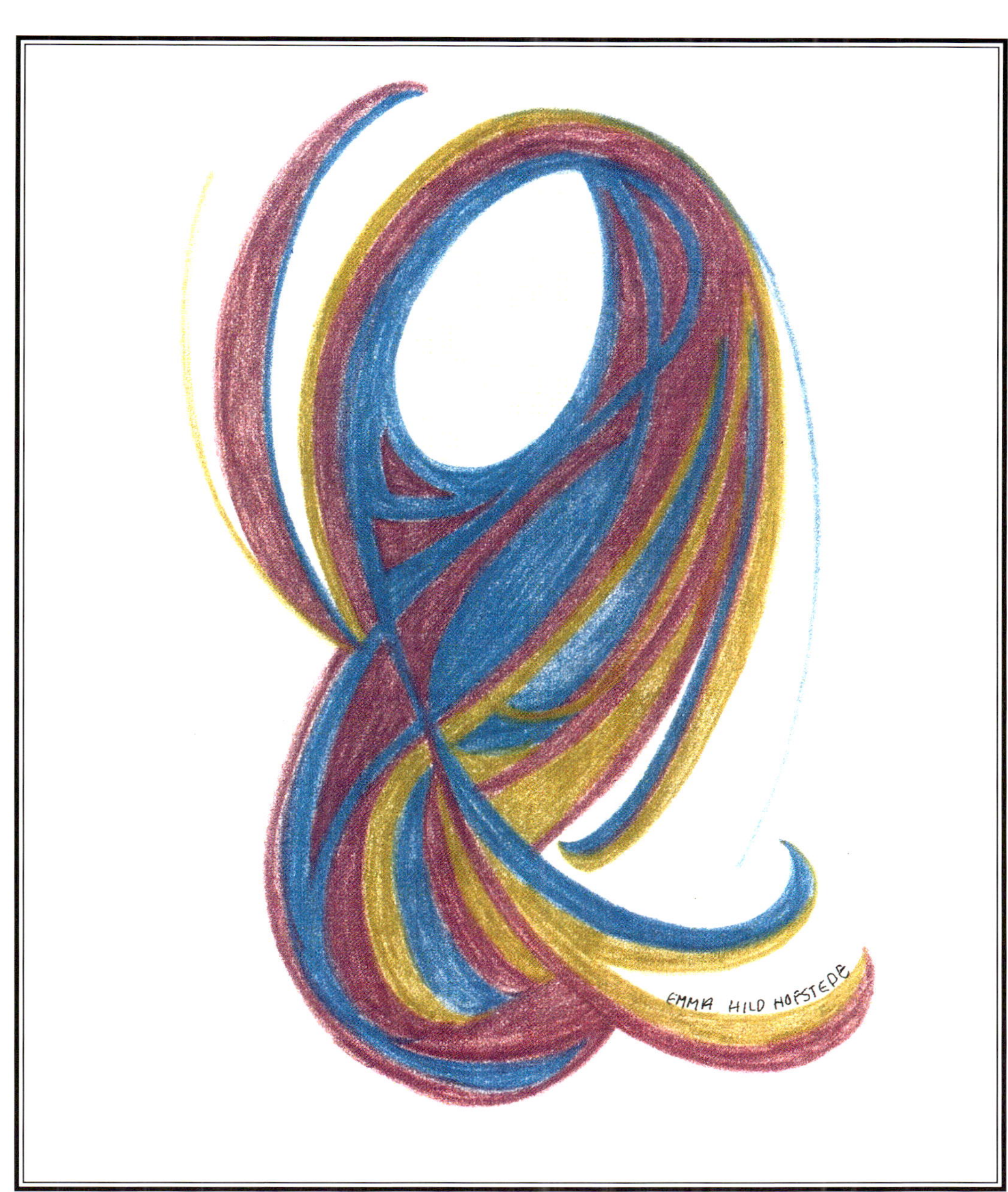
EMMA HILD HOFSTEDE

Quiet Intimacy

The woods behind our house are jungle lush. You couldn't walk through them right now if you wanted to. It is like they have closed in on themselves to hold close a sacred place for the animals and birds to nest and reproduce. In the other three seasons, you can see the deer and turkeys run through the forest.

Could it be the same for us? Do we have a place inside of us that closes over in lushness where we can rest in our own inner garden? Do we long for a place apart where we can meet with our God?

Nature mirrors so much for us about relationships. There is really no one who does not want a touch of God. We are made that way. A part of us remembers the time before our earth presence. We are never disconnected from our spirit home. The door is right inside of you where the fountain of your breath rises up carrying you and God out into the world. Isn't that wonderful!

"It's Not About the Horse"

This is the title of a book written by Wyatt H. Webb with Andy Pearlman. You don't need to read the book to understand the meaning of the title. A friend told me about it, and then Grandmother God wanted to know what it was about. I told her different groups come to a ranch for a week and are each given a horse. They are responsible for its care. During the time they are there, they talk about their feeling about the horse.

What the author discovered was that whatever characteristics the person found in their horse, they were different than what other people experienced working with the same horse. Thus the conclusion, it's not about the horse.

Grandmother God loved it. What a wonderful way to move away from projection or blaming of others for what is within our own selves. She thought this would even get God off the hook. People often accuse God of sending hard things to people to test them. Who could love a God like this?

We talked about examples that would illustrate how this works. Just think of someone who has a characteristic that annoys you. Like let's say the horse (person) was uncooperative. If you hold that feeling, and look at it like a jewel, you will see where in your own life you are uncooperative. When you are able to acknowledge it might be about you, the horse is free of your projection. If you claim it as yours, you can change it.

EMMA HILD HOFSTEDE

Miracles

It is raining here at the lake cabin; one of those gentle rains that sounds like music with a soft comforting rhythm. Grandmother God and I are sitting on the porch having a cup of mango tea and cozying up for a chat.

I asked Grandmother God what she thought about miracles. She just looked at me, and said, "What about them?" "Well is there such a thing, like people instantly getting well?" I said, "When Jesus lived they seemed to happen all the time." She knew that I was asking about this because my friend's son was having serious surgery next Tuesday.

Grandmother God always hesitates before she says something. "Honey," she said, "The love we have for one another is a power far greater than you realize. It can change almost anything. When lots of people pray, the energy intensifies all the more. Remember when all the people gathered in the hospital when your husband was having surgery? You could feel it couldn't you? We make such a huge difference to one another. We can radiate love and healing energy with our intention. What miracle occurs is not always clear. But one does happen."

"I know you are wondering why people do not get well. It is always your question because of your dear friend Ann. She totally believed in healing. What was healed was her heart, not her body. She wants you to know that. Believe in the healing power of prayer and intention. It is our gift to one another."

I told Grandmother God I asked a friend if she believed in miracles, and my friend said a wonderful thing. She said, "We are the messengers of healing. We carry this loving energy to one another like Jesus did when he lived on earth. His presence radiated a healing energy so powerful he could work miracles." Grandmother God said, "We carry that power."

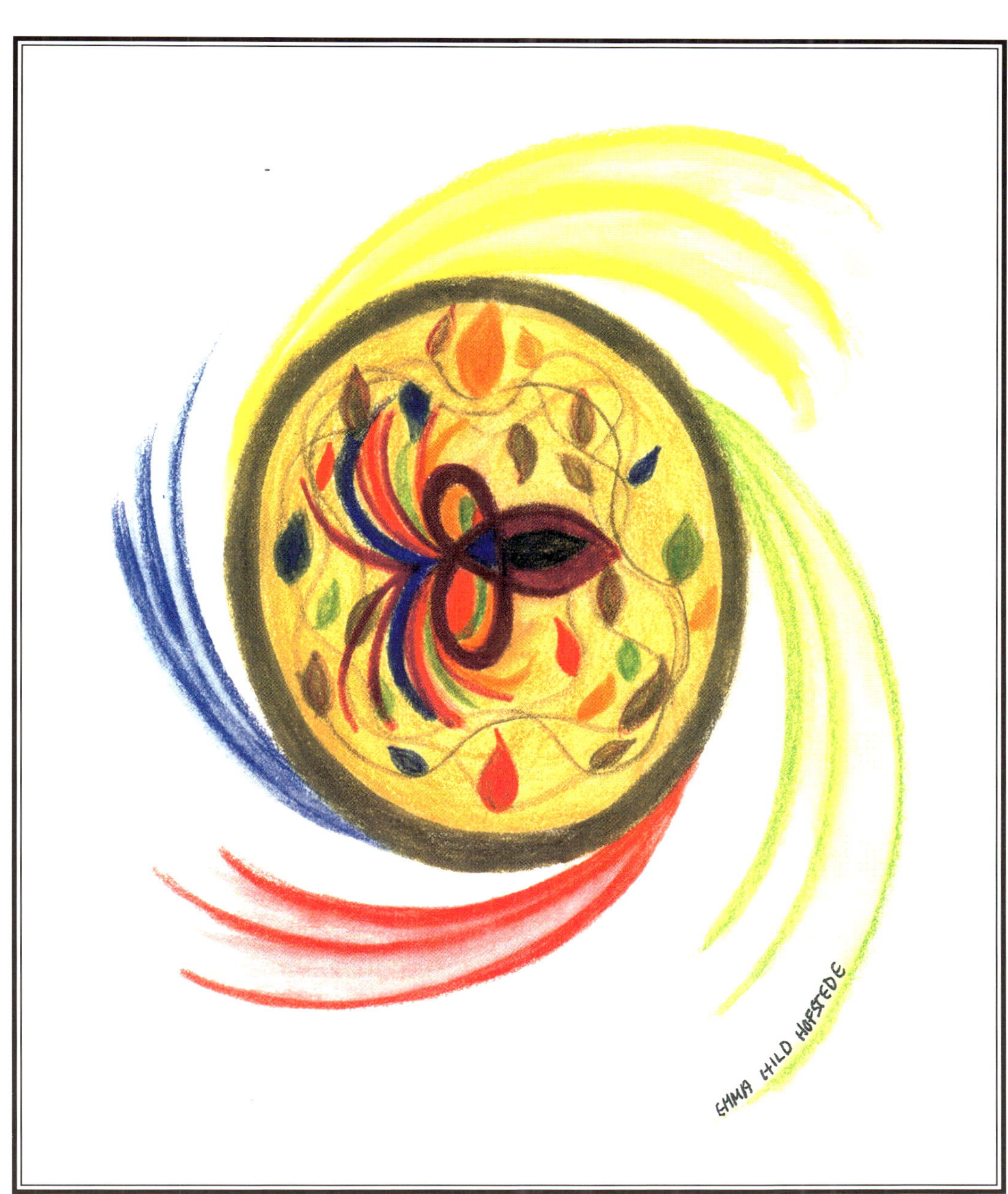

EMMA HILD HOFSTEDE

Being Real

Grandmother God thinks we will start growing feathers pretty soon up here in the Northland. She is getting pretty tired of the cold and damp weather. I asked her what exactly were her powers on Earth, and she told me that changing the weather was not one of them. Grandmother God came to share our experiences. She has some pretty spiffy comments about most things.

Her opinion of nice is that it can get in the way of being real. She thinks there are times for nice, but not 24/7. Being real is a full-time job. I asked her how that works when saying how you feel could be risky.

"Emma, let's have some tea and talk about this. If you are not true to yourself, who will be? Who will speak for the soft center of your being? Who will protect that sweetness that does not have her own voice? I know it is pretty hard to be real when someone is saying hurtful things. You don't have to react to the words, but you do have to turn inward and tell your sweet self that you will care for her, that you will do whatever it takes. The wonderful thing about this is that only you can do it for yourself. You do not have to wait for anyone else. They have their own lives, and their own sweet selves to love. It is up to you to make it a lovely dwelling place for yourself."

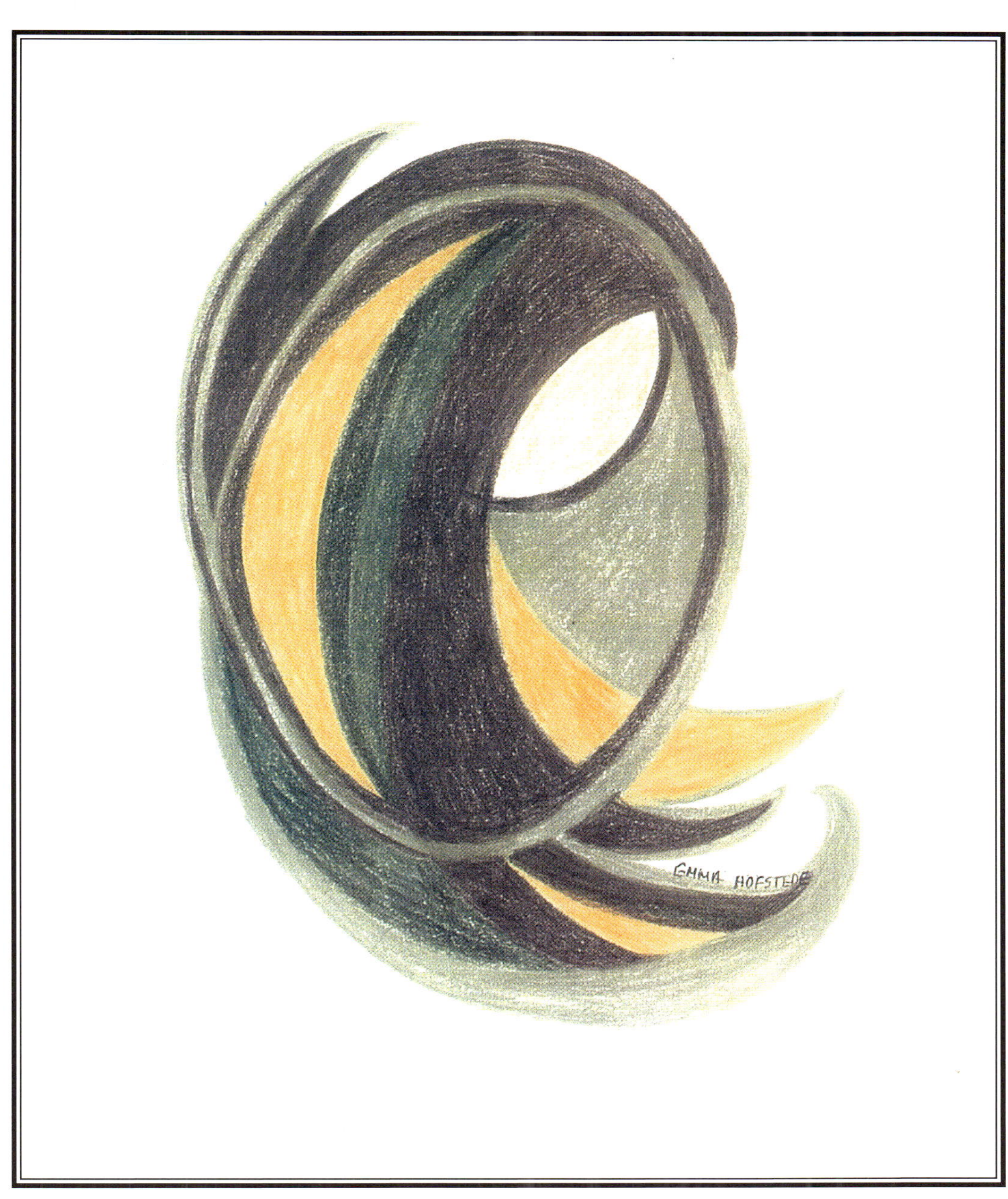
GEMMA HOFSTEDE

Wedding Love

Grandmother God loves weddings. She likes to dress up; she has a lovely blue dress just for this kind of occasion. What is so special for her about being around this much love is that it is contagious. Everyone attending the wedding comes with such good wishes, and the entire bridal party glows and sparkles with love.

We arrived with plenty of time to get good seats and watch the people coming in. We also had time to talk with our friends. There is something so special about the atmosphere around a wedding, and this one had it in spades.

The bride wore her mother's own wedding dress that she had made for her own wedding. The bride also wore her mother's veil. What a sweet symbol of the love her parents have for each other carried on in the wedding of her daughter. Grandmother God thought this was beyond lovely.

The bride and groom wrote their own wedding vows. A hush spread throughout the church as they spoke these words of love and promise.

Grandmother God was overjoyed in this atmosphere of pure love. She sat there with a smile on her face that reflected the beauty and the joy of the occasion.

It was a wonderful experience for all of us and I know Grandmother God will be talking about this to her friends for a long time to come. She sent oodles of love to the bride and groom in the church as her wedding present. What a wonderful wedding.

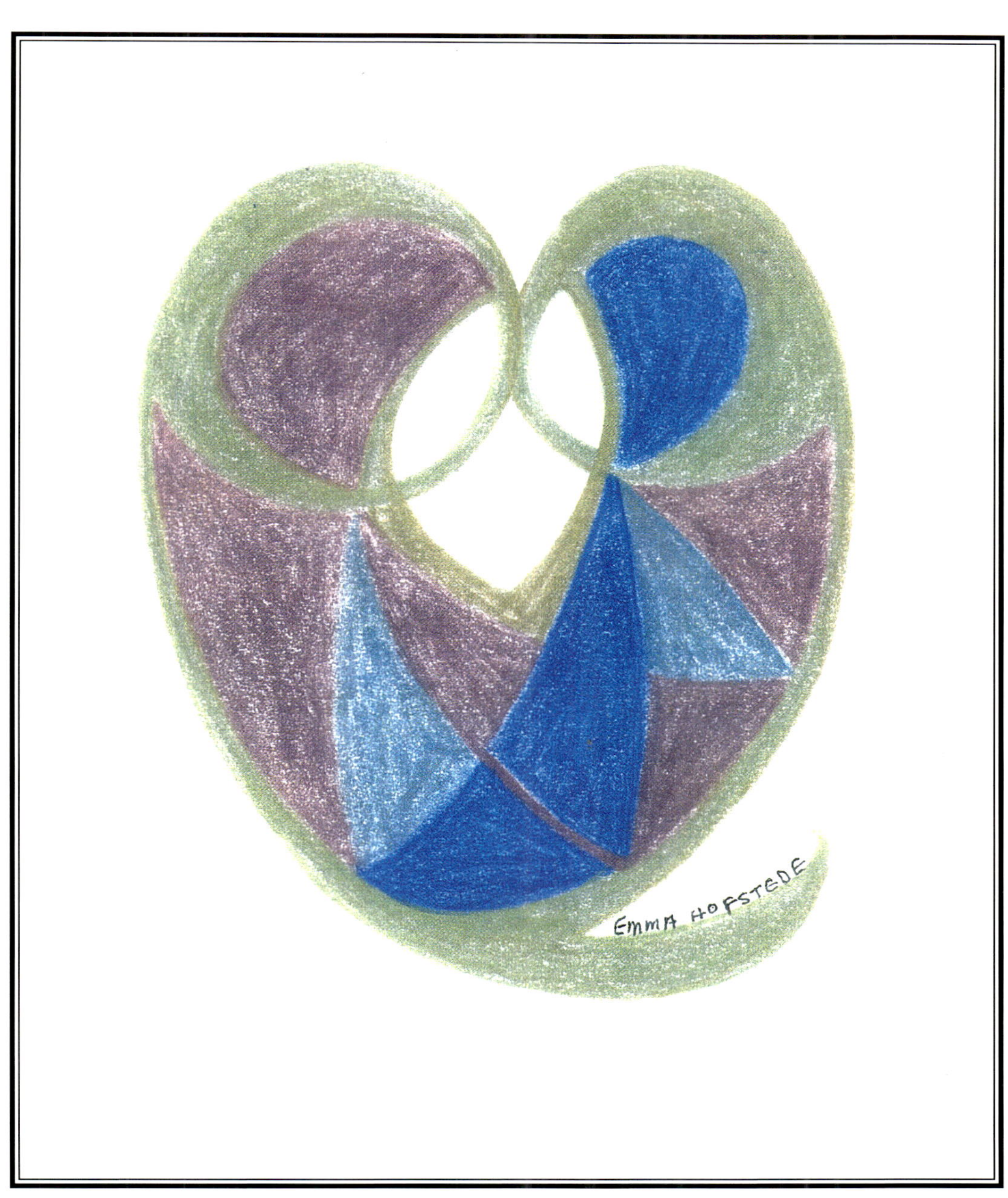
EMMA HOFSTEDE

The Heart's Rock

Can you imagine that when you are in need of comfort God would offer a rock to rest your heart on? In Psalm 73 that is exactly what is suggested.

"Though my flesh and my heart waste away,
God is my heart's rock and my portion forever."

Can you see your heart resting on a rock safe and secure in the warm sun? Grandmother God loves this image. At first we both thought it would be pretty uncomfortable to put your heart on a rock, but really how safe our sweet feelings would be resting right on God.

The juxtaposition of these two images shows us that there is no end to the ways that God tries to let us know how much we are loved and cherished.

The emotional core image of this Psalm is how close God is to us, and this feeling can sustain and give us the sense of being protected and loved.

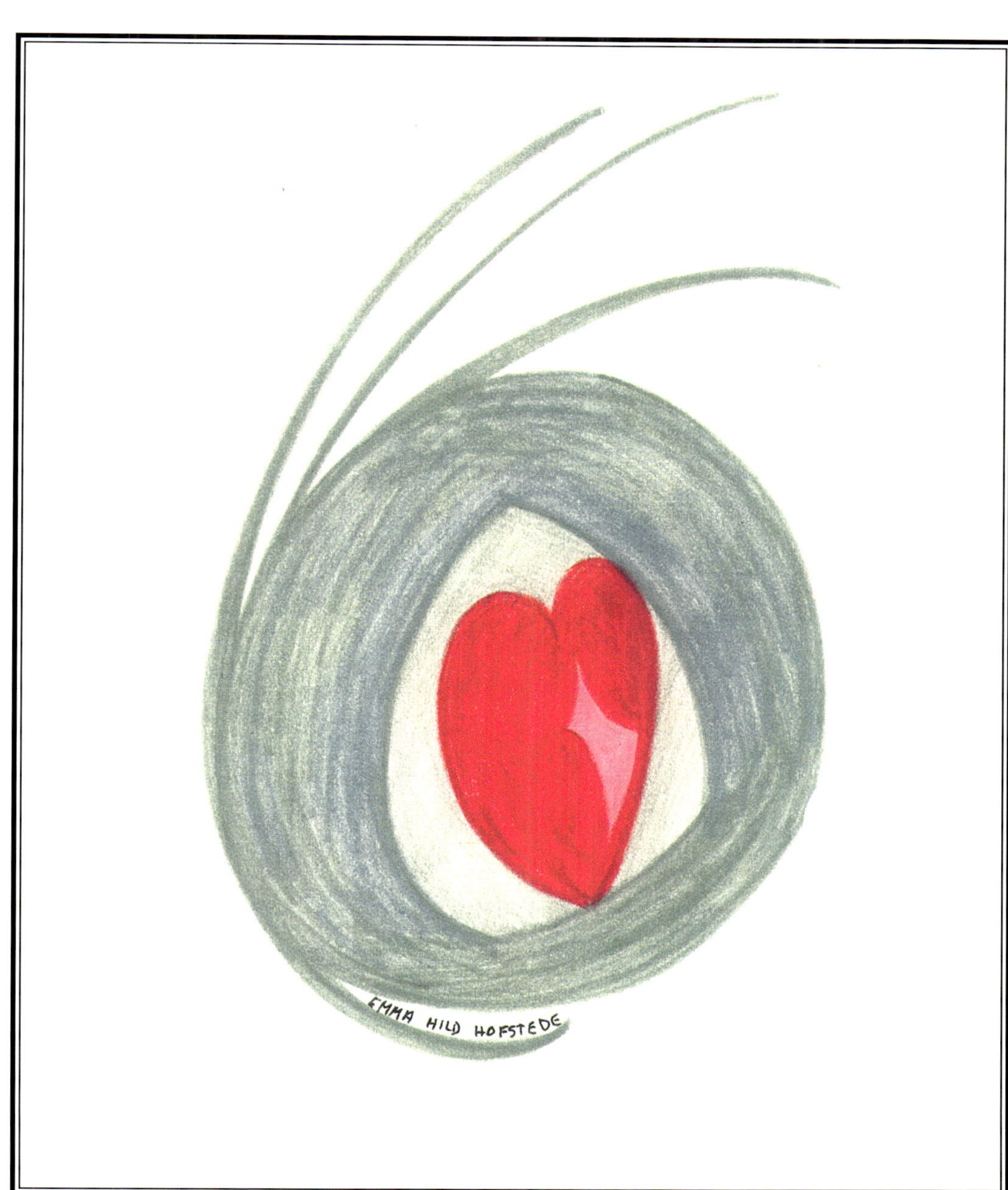
EMMA HILD HOFSTEDE

Grandmother God's
Message of Love to You

You are God's Beloved.
You are a vibration of love.
God calls you love.
God and you are one.

"All of your life you are searching for who you are, and what you are called to do on this earth. I want to tell all of you that your spirits are so radiant, that if you could only see each other you would be blinded by the beauty. When you are on earth, you have chosen to keep your glorious Self hidden. You have had moments when you can feel yourself glowing and feel it in others. Hold them close.

"I am here to remind all of you who you are. There are so many ways that living on this earth can cause you to not remember. I know who you are, and I can see you. I will help you when others for some reason or other try to blind you to yourself. You are a part of God. How could you be anything but beautiful?

"I have noticed since I have come with this message, that those who have gotten to know me are growing more and more in love. They do have their moments of fear and doubt, but love is contagious. I have come to start an epidemic.

"It is a lovely summer morning. I woke up with this message pressing on my heart. I wanted Emma to write it as soon as she got up.

"When you look in the mirror see the beauty, see your self. Speak with kind words to your magnificent being.

"You could even give your Self a little kiss."

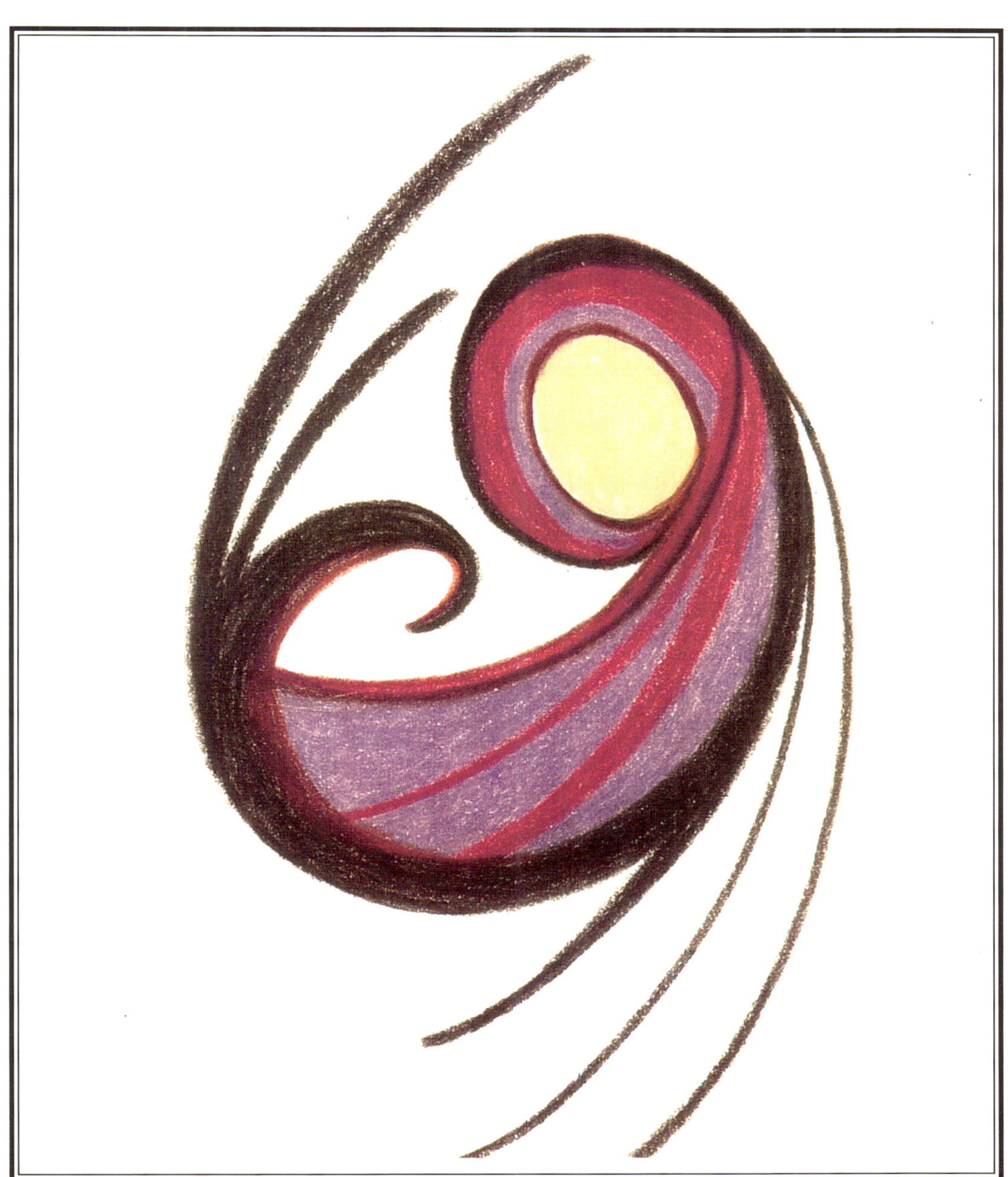

Feelings

Remember the morning Grandmother God was crying? She was mixing the color blue for the rainbow. Today I asked her what the other colors meant, and why the rainbow touches us all so deeply.

She said, "Feelings are like silken cords that connect us to each other." I told Grandmother God that today I was feeling hurt. She said, "Honey, let's paint the purple in the rainbow so you can honor your feeling. It is the tender part of you. Let's be gentle with it and let it sing across the sky."

Have you ever noticed how people will run outside when it is raining and the sun is shining? They are anxious to see and delight in the possibility of a rainbow. It still signals the song of hope God planted in our hearts.

Grandmother God says that she is in our feelings. When you tell someone how you feel, they can't help but feel closer to you. Their own silken thread entwines with yours. It is how we connect with one another. Expressing your feelings with a loved one creates intimacy.

You can wrap yourself in this glorious cloak of rainbow colors today, and paint your own feelings across the sky.

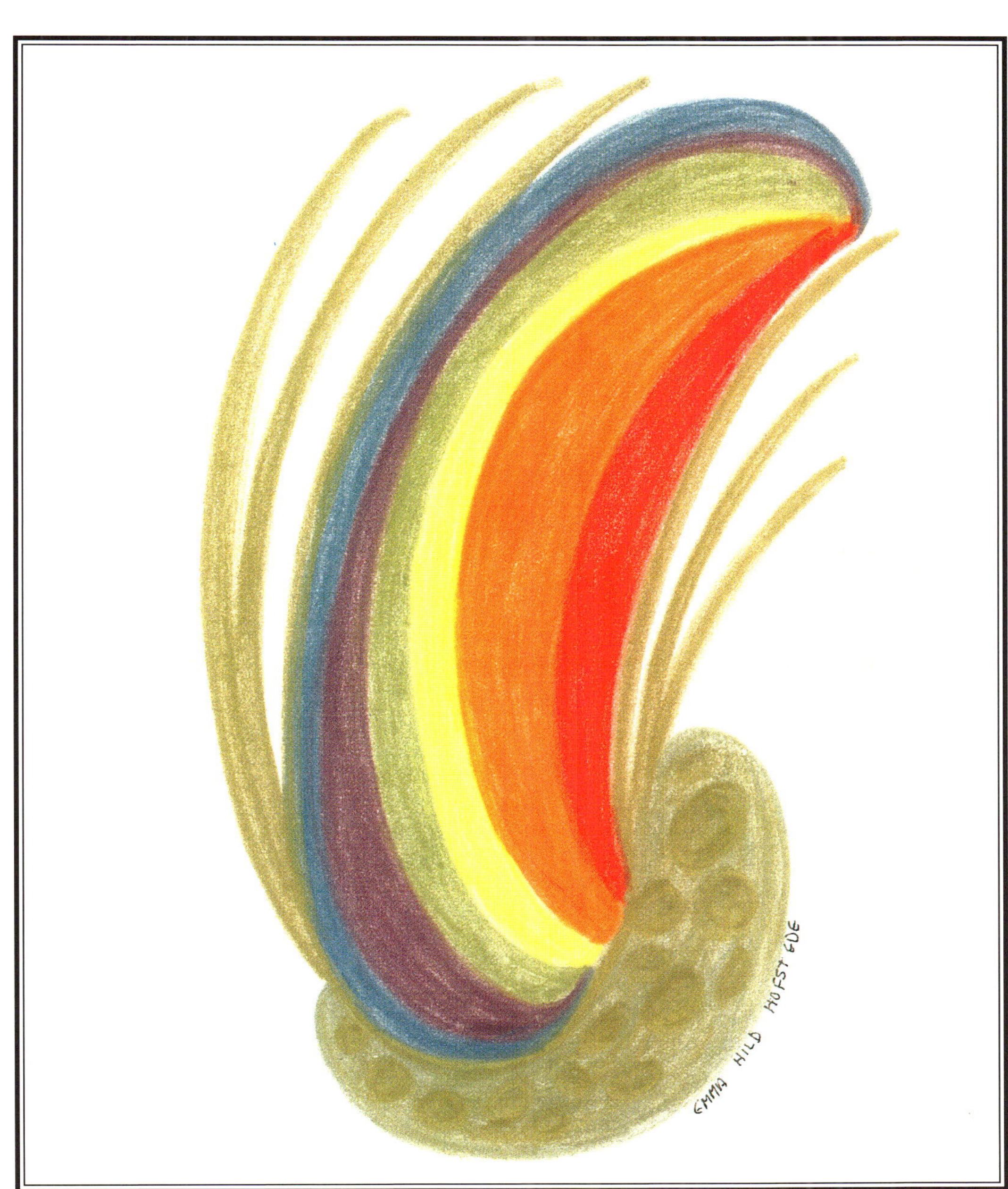
EMMA HILD HOFST 6DE

Good News

Yesterday we heard alarming news about my husband. The radiologist saw a spot on his lung. We will go see the oncologist this morning. The doctor said it was too small to tell yet what it is; however, it is not too small to scare the living daylights out of all of us.

Let me tell you something about Grandmother God. She is both a rock and a marshmallow. She stands firm, and at the same time her sweetness just flows out in tears and hugs. Her face lights up like the sun. Her love energy fills you, and when that happens, you feel better.

She saddled right up to my side this week while we were waiting for news about my husband. We were worried that the cancer had returned. What we found out was he had pneumonia. When we heard this news we were ecstatic. Pneumonia never sounded so good!

Grandmother God is the best to be with in this kind of situation. When she heard the news she hopped and skipped, and spun around thanking God. Now figure that one out. She grabbed my hands and looked into my eyes, and I never felt closer to anyone in all my life. She is pure love. I know she was showing me how we can do this for each other during difficult times. Our presence means so much, and she is saying never underestimate this power of love we carry inside of us.

Whenever you call her, she will come. "Prayers and love," she says, "That's what does it."

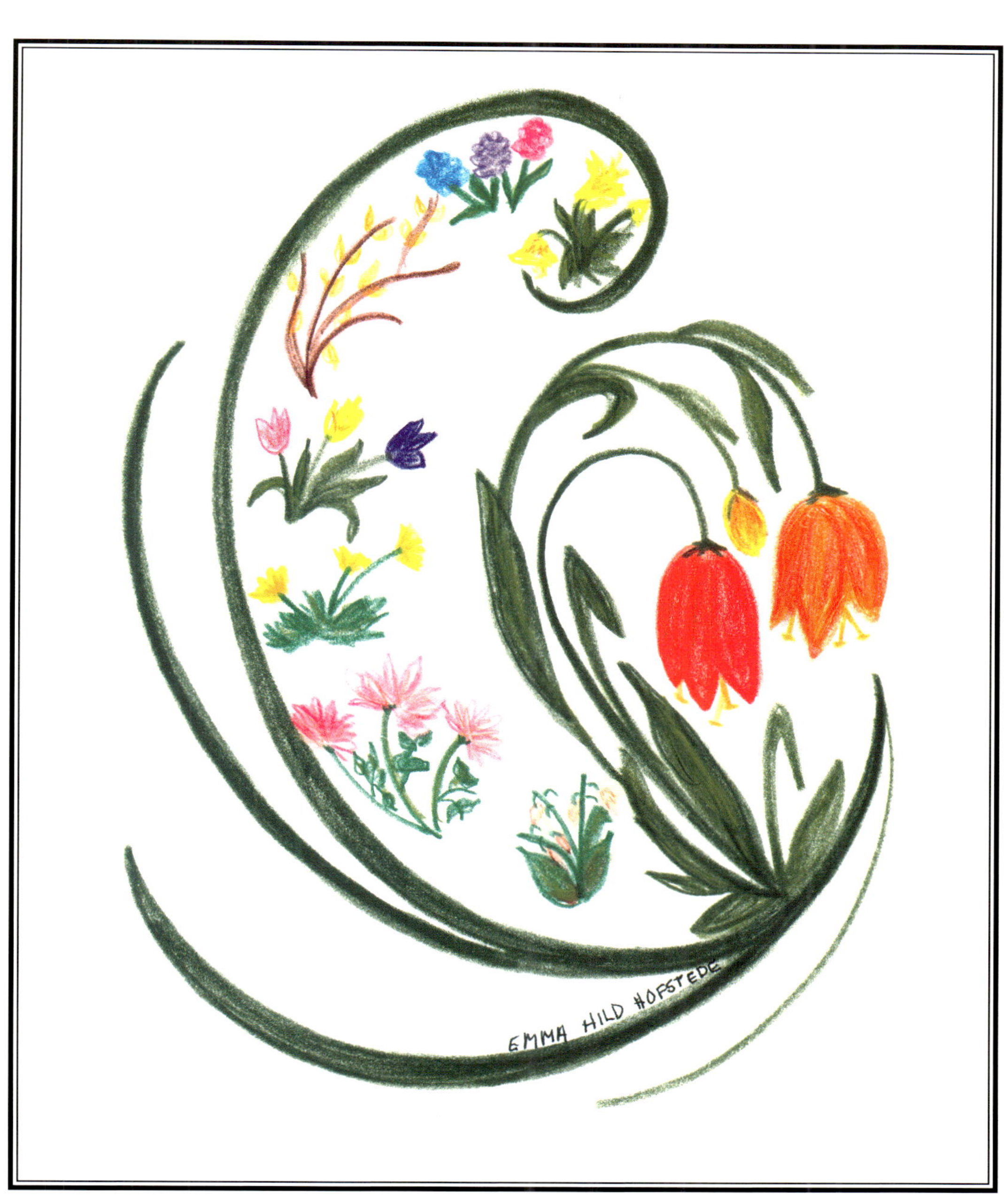

EMMA HILD HOFSTEDE

Robe of Joy

This morning Grandmother God found a wonderful phrase in Psalm 30.

> "You turned my dirge to a dance for me,
> undone my sackcloth and wrapped me with joy."

This Psalm talked about being wrapped in joy. It said that God pulls tight the garment of joy around us. We both thought that was a beautiful image of how much we are cared for and loved by God. Imagine the feeling of a beautiful robe of joy that was hanging in your closet. You could wear it whenever you wanted to feel a sense of joy, hope and a sense of the closeness of God's presence.

Remember that wonderful feeling of a warm wrap around you when you felt chilly? It is almost like you are able to give yourself a little hug along with the warmth. God's cloak is spun with joy. It is hard to imagine what that would feel and look like.

Sometimes it is hard to recall this wonderful image of the cloak of joy, when life bears down upon us. Grandmother God knows this, and wants you to turn to her as soon as we lose the feeling of her presence. She will be right there helping us to remember to put on that beautiful joyful cloak and wrapping it around our shoulders.

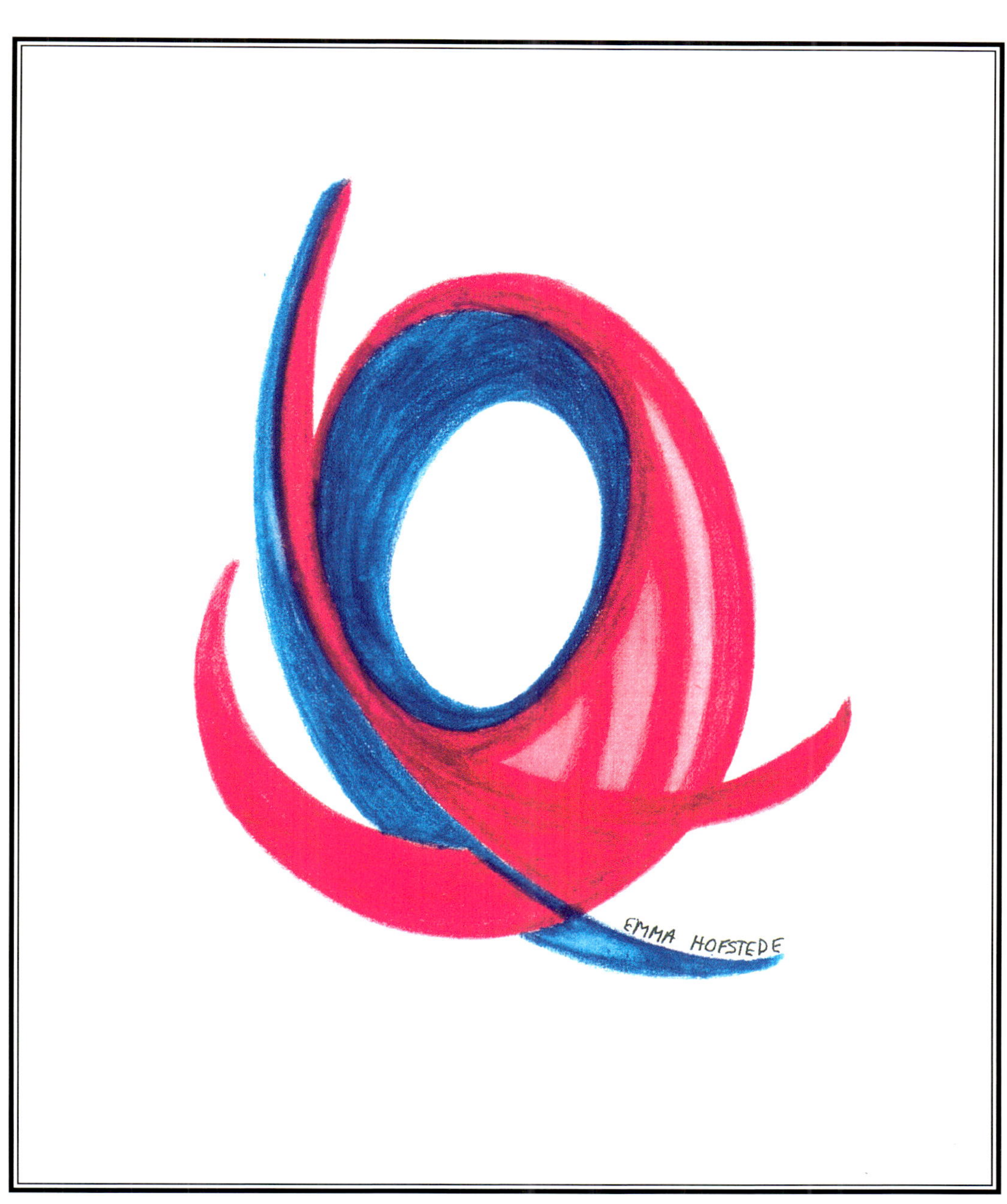
EMMA HOFSTEDE

Gathering of Tears

It is a cool summer morning. Grandmother God and I are sitting on the porch drinking mango tea and talking. The woods are so lush that you feel like you are in paradise. The Japanese lilacs are in bloom and the fragrance fills the air. It doesn't get much better than this.

This morning we were reading Psalm 56:

> ". . . put my tears in Your flask.
> are they not in your counting?"

The footnote tells of a compassionate God gathering the tears of the sufferer in a celestial flask and counting every one of them.

We both loved that image of a God who would count your tears, and be that close to you. When you cry, God gathers them in a flask and counts them. Grandmother God says that is what she wants us to know. You are loved this much, tended to this much by God. My experience of living with Grandmother God fits right into this image. She doesn't use a flask, but she is sitting right beside you when you cry, or laugh, or you are just being yourself.

She said maybe she would get a flask. She likes the idea of gathering the tears and counting them. I have to remind her this is 2009.

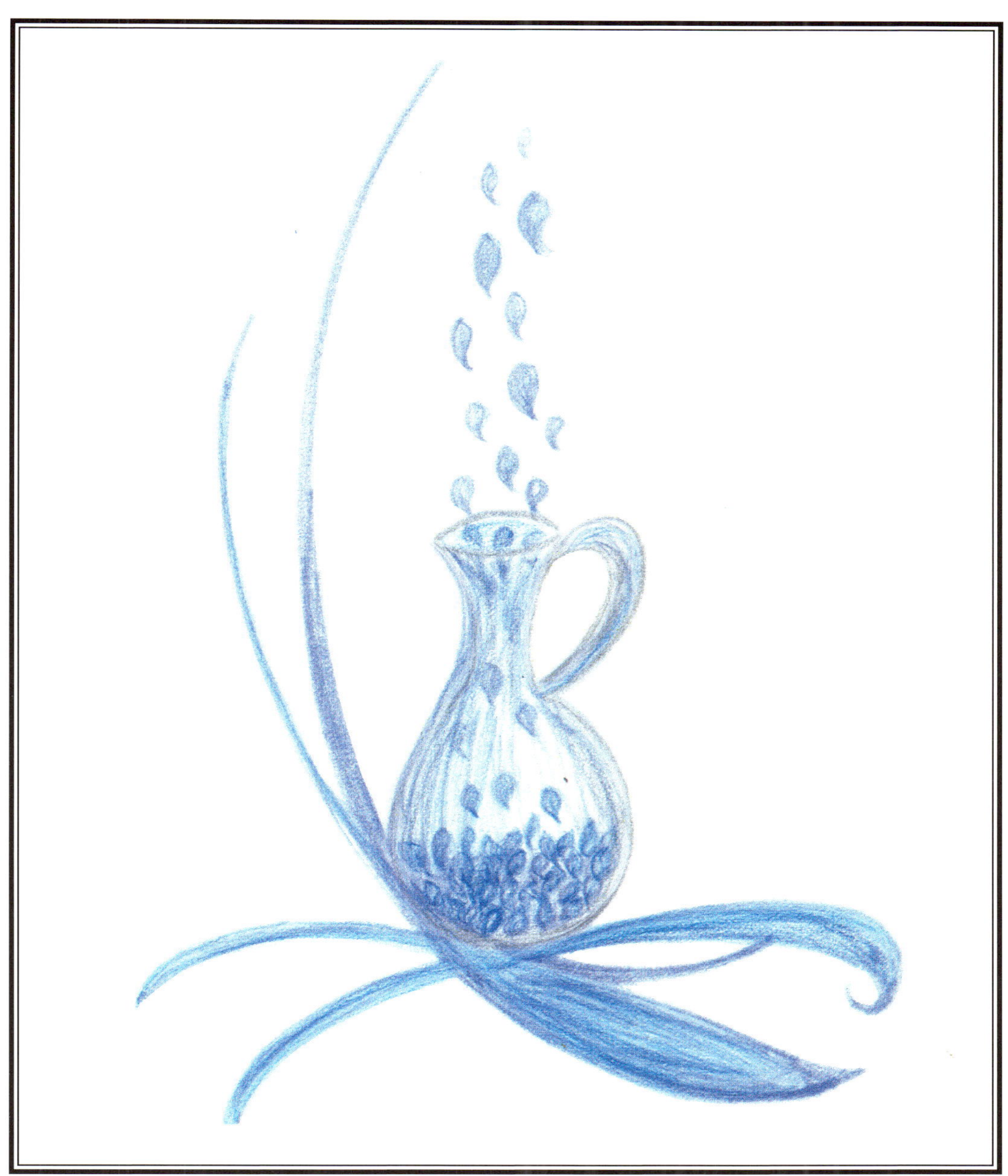

Surrender to Love

Wе are going home today from the cabin, enough time here, and too many bats. Grandmother God insisted that I write this before we left.

She wanted to meet in "The Inner Room." It was the place I first met her. I could see the lights under the door. When she chose this place to talk, I knew she had something really important to say for the end of our book. She cut right to the chase, not even any tea.

I don't know about you, but surrender has never been one of my favorite words. I have associated surrender with submission, and I think that for women, and men too, that is a hard concept.

It is something I don't think of too often. In these last few years there have been so many difficult things in my life, and in the lives of my friends. Surrender is not the first thing I think of to cope. Mostly it is relying on grace, and getting through it. Lately I have become more aware of surrender as the jewel of love. This morning I knew that Grandmother God was going to go right to the surrender piece.

Sure enough, she started off with, "Emma," and I knew then she was going to talk to me about something that she wanted in her book. So here it is. "Surrender is about your love relationship with God. It is only God that can offer the love and trust you need for this complete immersion into love." I knew Grandmother God was serious about this message. She leaned closer to me and looked into my eyes with such love that my heart started to melt. She knew she had me.

Grandmother God said, "Emma, close your eyes and imagine yourself falling into a deep flowing stream. You are leaving your familiar shore. You are floating backwards. You are afraid. You realize that you are not actually floating, but someone is holding you up and you are leaning back into a Presence, like you are floating on a raft." Grandmother God stops here, and looks at me. I know she is seeing if I am getting this. She knows how I feel about surrender. I smile, and she continues.

"This is what surrendering to love is, Emma. You lean back with complete trust and love in God who is sustaining you. This is about your spirit, and how it never left God when you were born, and never will be separated at death. When you took on a

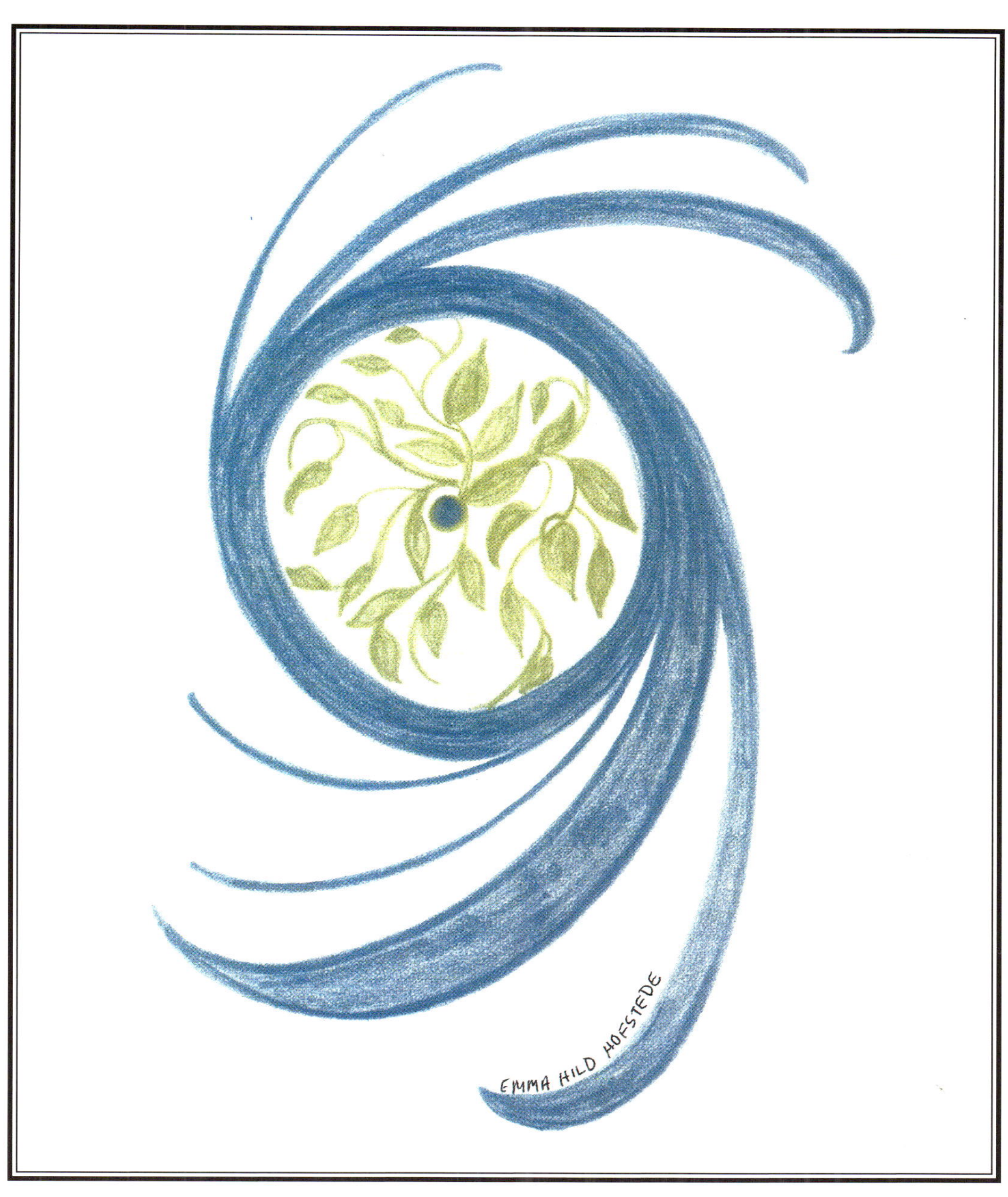
EMMA HILD HOFSTEDE

human form, it's the part of you that walks the shores of earth encountering all kinds of wonderful and difficult things. All the while, you live in the Inner Room, in God's arms, the stream is a metaphor for your life. It is full of currents and rapids, but you are never alone. When you know this, you can enjoy the ride, and become more aware of all the sights and sounds of your journey. Emma, I will never let you down." She smiles at her pun.

"In closing, my dear ones, remember your breath, my breath is within your breath, breathing you, and the flowing river of life, the place where we surrender to each other in a complete love union. The secret is that God breathes you, and you breathe God. In the river, God holds you up, and you bring God to the surface in our world. I saved the best piece for last. Isn't that beautiful!" She smiles and hugs me, and she hugs you too.

Epilogue

THE UPPER ROOM

It is a beautiful September morning. The woods are filled with white wild flowers. The sunlight is not like the brilliant splashes of summer light; rather it spreads softness over the profusion of flowers.

I miss Grandmother God so much. She no longer sits with me and talks and has tea. Her work is finished here, and I feel like she disappeared gradually. I realized just these last few weeks that she was no longer here in the same way. I would have liked a good-bye, but maybe that would have been too hard. A friend of mine wondered if it wasn't how the Apostles of Jesus felt when he left.

It was in a dream I had in August that she reappeared. She was sitting at a table in an Upper Room with two other women. I drove to a high rise on a lake, and went to the top floor. A woman answered the door and invited me in to join them around a table. I knew who they were. Of course I recognized Grandmother God, and I knew the other two were Mary, and a Spirit filled with light. I was asked to come back as they were not quite ready for me. So I did, and this time I brought bread, honey, sweet butter, and strawberry jam. I sat down with them, and Grandmother God broke the bread and we all took a piece and ate together.

It is only now that I am realizing the significance of that dream. Grandmother God calls us all to that place of complete love inside of us. In the Inner Room, only Grandmother God was present, but here in the Upper Room the fullness of God lives, and we are welcomed right into this center. It is the conclusion of her message. Love lives within us, and we live within this love. It is her parting gift to all of us, and I pass it on to you, her dear friends.

EMMA HILD HOFSTEDE